CARAVAGGIO:
juego de manos
Galería

Editorial Persona
Dirección Postal
Matías Montes, Presidente
9759 NW 30 St. Doral, FL. 33172
Dirección electrónica
mmhuidobro@aol.com

Copyright © Matías Montes Huidobro

Primera Edicion, Editorial Persona, 2017

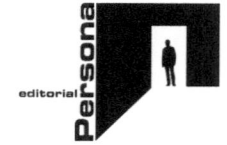

GF Graphic Design
Diseño de cubierta y páginas interiores:
Luis G. Fresquet
www.fresquetart.com
luisgfresq@gmail.com

Un proyecto de Pro Teatro Cubano

ISBN-13: 978-1979383738

ISBN-10: 1979383731

Está prohibida la reproducción total o parcial de esta obra sin la autorización de Editorial Persona,

CARAVAGGIO:
juego de manos

Galería

Matías Montes Huidobro

LIBRO TERCERO

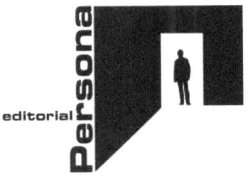

PALABRAS PRELIMINARES

por Matías Montes Huidobro

Caravaggio: juego de manos es posiblemente el más difícil y complicado de todos mis libros. Tomando como punto de partida la obra de Caravaggio, comprende el análisis de un total de setenta y cinco reproducciones en colores de su obra plástica, lo que ya, de por sí, es excepcional, en una constante interacción entre vida y obra que navega entre la novela y el ensayo. El propósito inmediato de esta *Galería*, no es otro que darle al lector una opción adicional para llevar a efecto la lectura de *Caravaggio: juego de manos*, con el texto en una mano y el añadido gráfico en colores en la otra. Aunque el texto literario existe en sí mismo y los dos volúmenes de la edición tienen una referencia visual en blanco y negro, no hay dudas que dado el caso de un pintor de la talla de Caravaggio y la naturaleza de mi propuesta, es conveniente tener a mano la imagen en colores, que forma parte del montaje visual y hasta fílmico que propone la narrativa. En realidad el proceso creador estuvo siempre acompañado de esta interacción, saltando del campo literario al pictórico, lo que colocaría al lector en la misma posición que adopté para escribir el libro. Los cuadros lo reubican dentro de esta circunstancia, que es también la del propio Caravaggio visto desde mi perspectiva analítica.

Tras la fúnebres circunstancias de la plaga durante su infancia, Roma viene a ser la guía del ocio de una picaresca callejera que es la llave que le abre la puerta al universo de la metrópoli urbana con las opciones de las comisiones públicas del discurso oficial y las colecciones privadas (del Monte, Guistiniani, Mattei), para los cuales Caravaggio representa el discurso transgresor de lo prohibido (Fillis, Anna Bianchini, Lena, Cecco) sin riesgo para ellos, lo cual nos permite proponer el esquema que sigue:

(MILÁN)

ROMA

Plaza del Popolo	Plaza de las Flores	Campo Marcio
	Ortazio	
	Tor di Nona	
	Cabeza de la Medusa	
Atalier Cavalier D'Arpino		Hospital de la Consolación
	Palacio Madama	

CARDENAL DEL MONTE

COLECCIONES PRIVADAS

Giustiniani, del Monte, Mattei

COMISIONES PÚBLICAS

San Luis	San Agustín	Santa Maria del Pópolo
Capilla Cotarelli		Capilla Cerasi
	Iglesia Nueva	
	Entierro de Cristo	

LOGROS Y RECHAZOS

Muerte de Ranuccio Tomasoni

"discurso masculino" "discurso homoerótico" "discurso femenino"

"discurso oficial" "discurso transgresor"

"discurso psíquico"

"discurso cristológico"

NÁPOLES

MALTA   SICILIA

ERCOLE

MUERTE Y RESURRECCIÓN

Merisi invita al gran espectáculo, un musical que no se ha llevado a escena todavía, o a un filme donde su vida se proyecte en pantalla con la presencia de los múltiples escenarios donde se desarrolló vida y obra: Milán, Caravaggio, Roma, Nápoles, Malta, Sicilia, Ercole. El recorrido visual reconfirma el punto de vista: la vida y obra de Caravaggio es un contrapunto callejero y sicológico con innumerables vericuetos que expanden las opciones más allá de sus propios límites.

Sirva la gráfica previa de síntesis de nuestra propuesta a partir de la plaga en Milán, parte esencial de un proceso plástico que lleva al desarrollo total que gesta a Caravaggio, para pasar al discurso colectivo de plazas y callejuelas que lo conducen metafóricamente a la Tor di Nona, (claustrofóbica, fálica y freudiana) donde la pintura elabora la Cabeza de la Medusa como discurso ofensivo y defensivo, que el pintor maneja como un espadachín apresado en su destino. El "discurso del natural" de los complejos primeros años en Roma lo conducirá al cambio de giro que representa el Palacio Madama, las comisiones privadas de del Monte, Guistiniani, Mattei y otros más, que conducen a las públicas de San Luigui, Santa María del Popolo, San Agustín, la Iglesia Nueva, etc., que determinarán su presencia hoy en día, entre logros y rechazos, en todos los museos del mundo. Al mismo tiempo, dramáticamente, lo conducirá al clímax del duelo con Tomassoni que todo lo trastoca. Del nudo al desenlace, del realismo al expresionismo transgresor, una serie de discursos configuran unidades de desarrollo, con una condición bíblica y evangélica, de lo oficial a lo transgresor, que nos lleva por el callejón sin salida: Nápoles, Malta, Sicilia, hasta el fatal desenlace en Ercole.

LIBRO PRIMERO

Galería

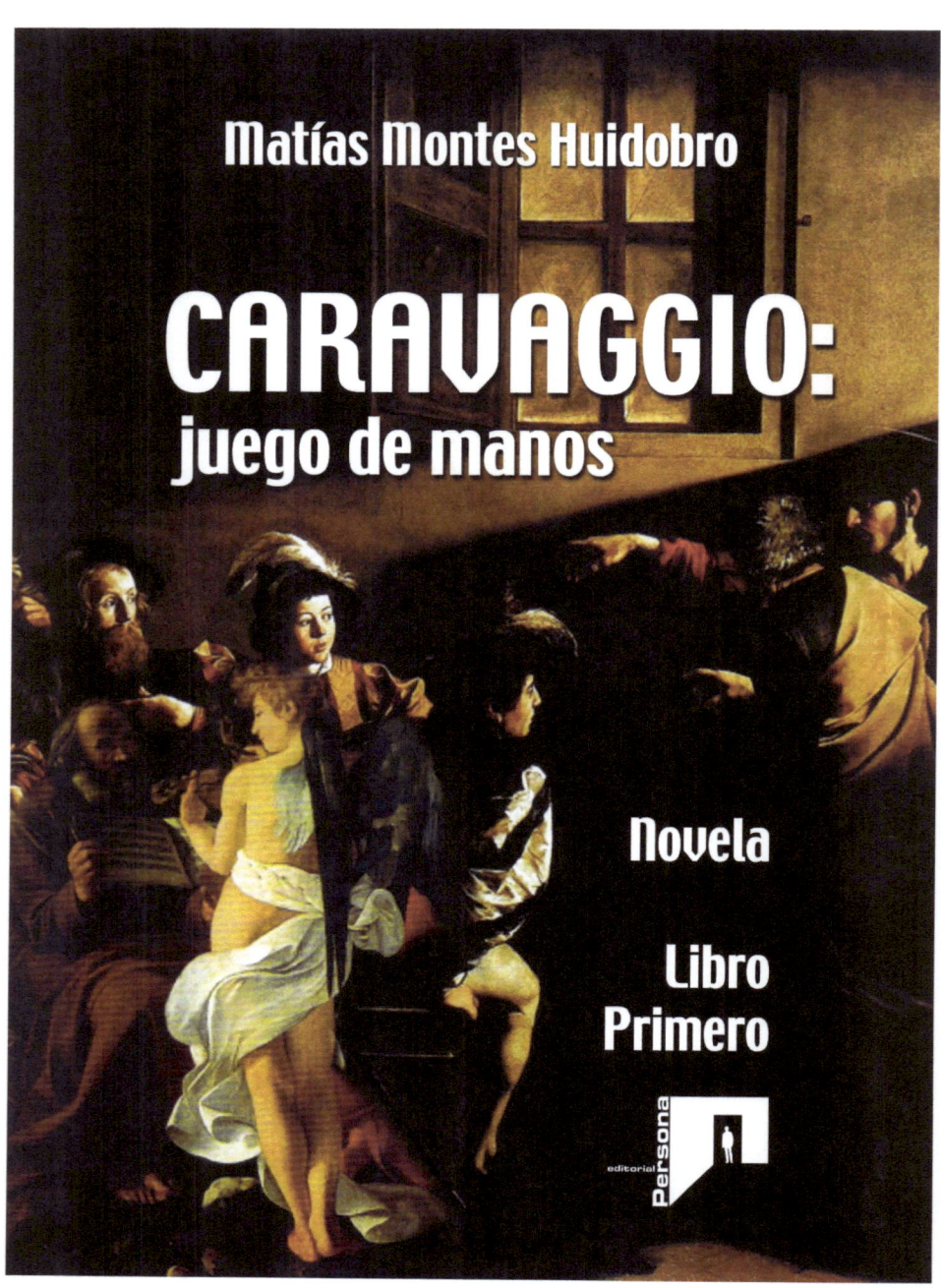

Portada y contra portada: Diseño de Luis García Fresquet

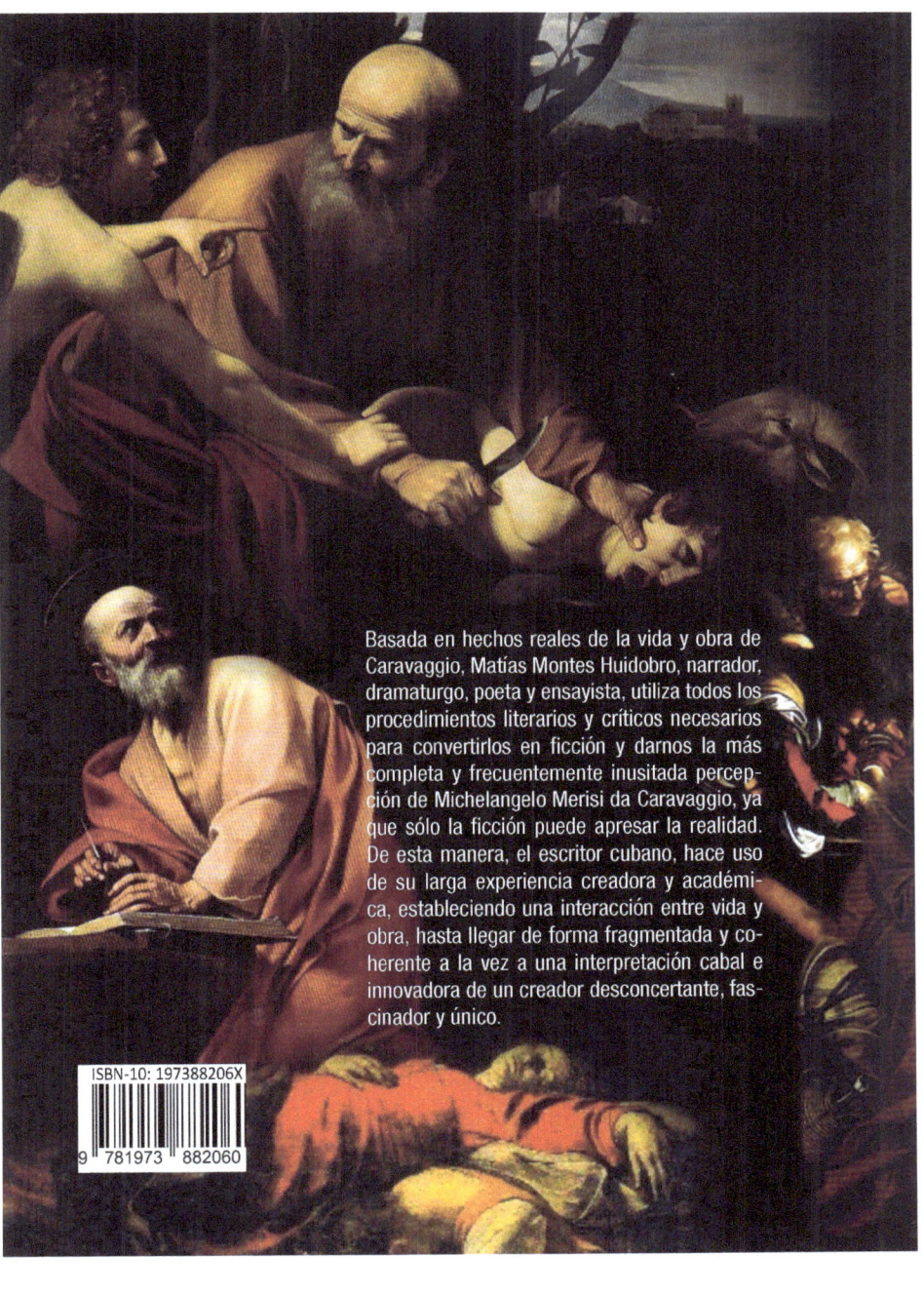

Basada en hechos reales de la vida y obra de Caravaggio, Matías Montes Huidobro, narrador, dramaturgo, poeta y ensayista, utiliza todos los procedimientos literarios y críticos necesarios para convertirlos en ficción y darnos la más completa y frecuentemente inusitada percepción de Michelangelo Merisi da Caravaggio, ya que sólo la ficción puede apresar la realidad. De esta manera, el escritor cubano, hace uso de su larga experiencia creadora y académica, estableciendo una interacción entre vida y obra, hasta llegar de forma fragmentada y coherente a la vez a una interpretación cabal e innovadora de un creador desconcertante, fascinador y único.

ISBN-10: 197388206X

9 781973 882060

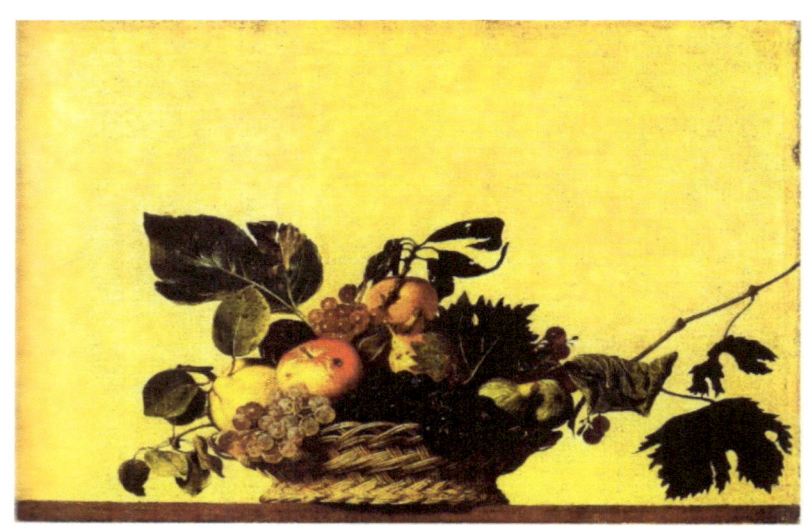

CESTA DE FRUTAS

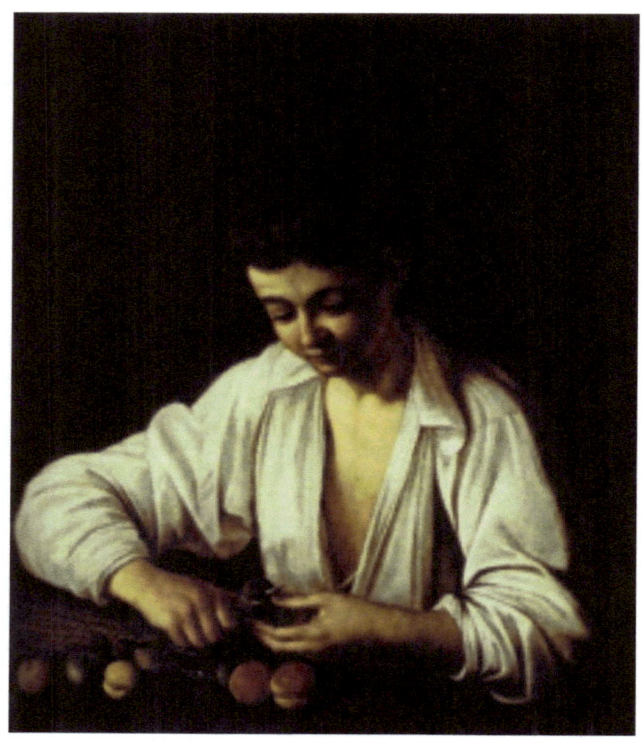

MUCHACHO PELANDO UN BERGAMOTO

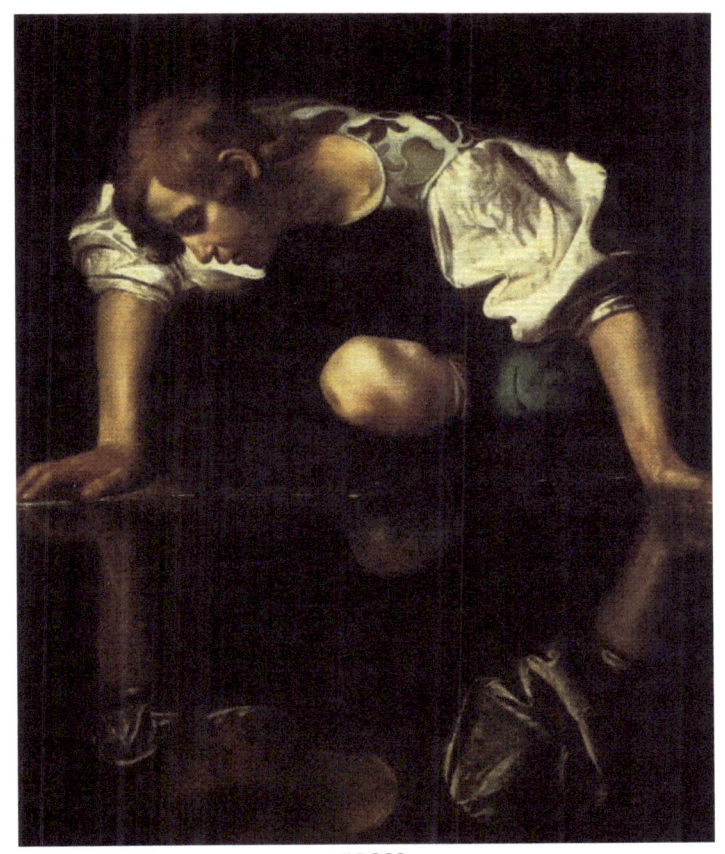

NARCISO

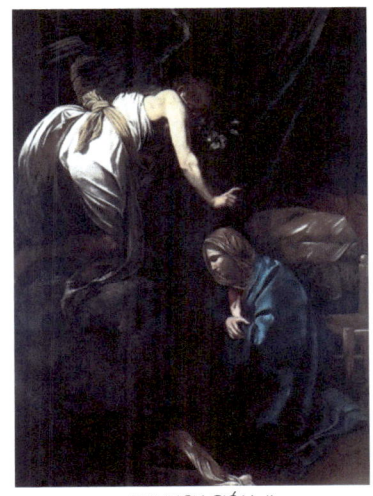

ANUNCIACIÓN II

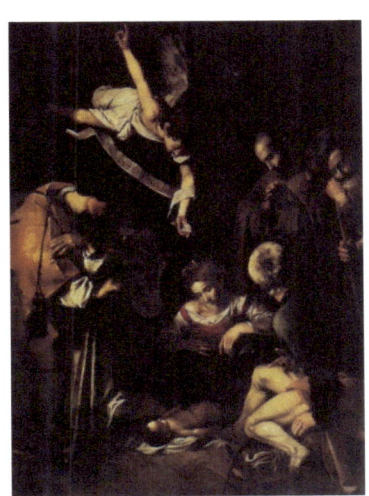

NATIVIDAD II

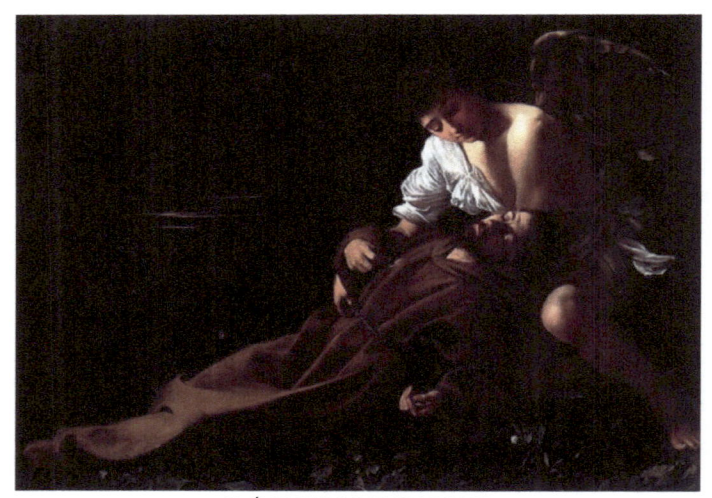

EL ÉXTASIS DE SAN FRANCISCO

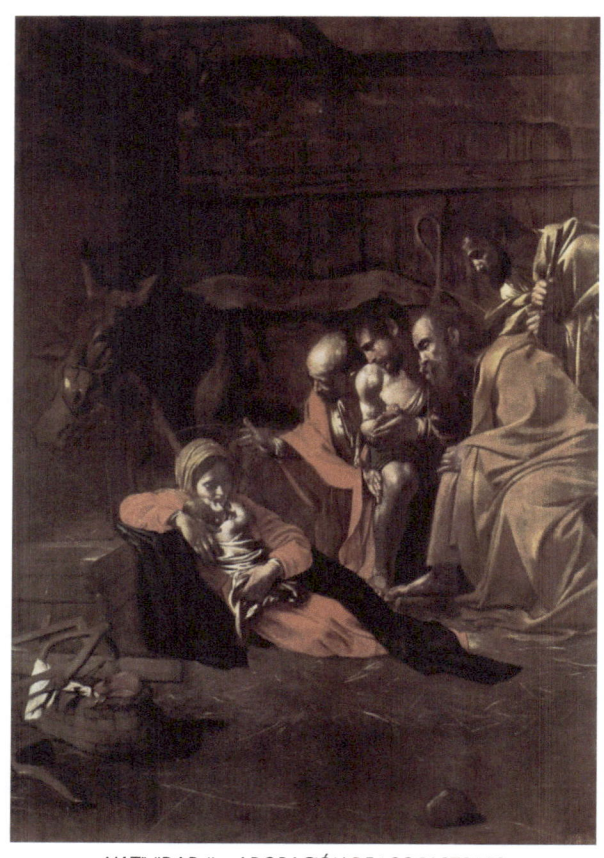

NATIVIDAD II   ADORACIÓN DE LOS PASTORES

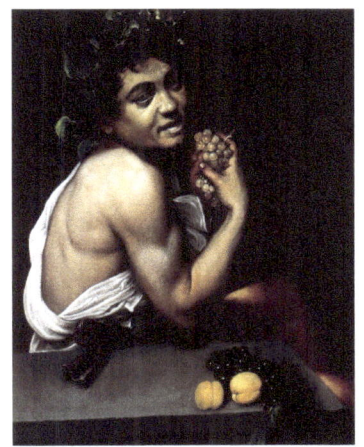
BACO ENFERMO

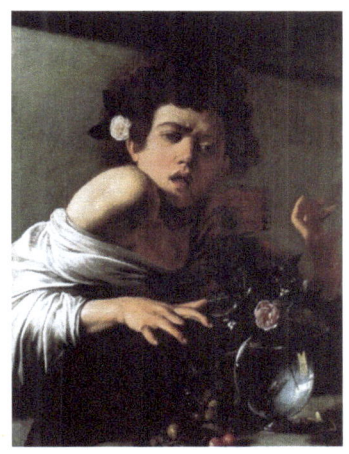
MUCHACHO MORDIDO POR UN LAGARTO

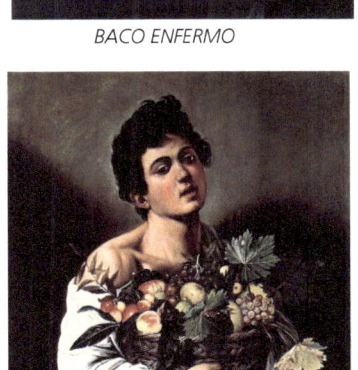
MUCHACHO CON CESTA DE FRUTAS

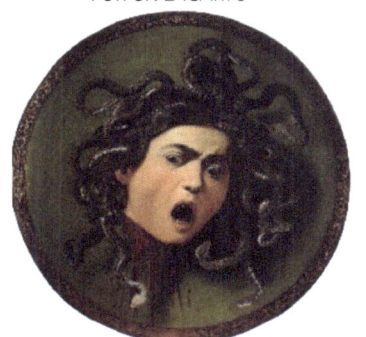
CABEZA DE LA MEDUSA

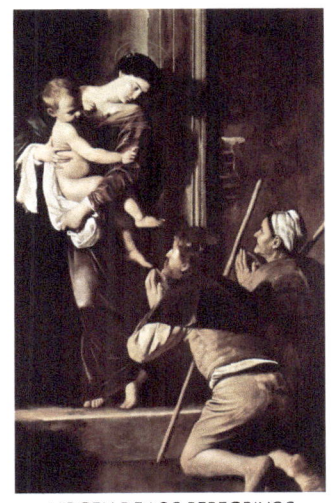
VIRGEN DE LOS PEREGRINOS

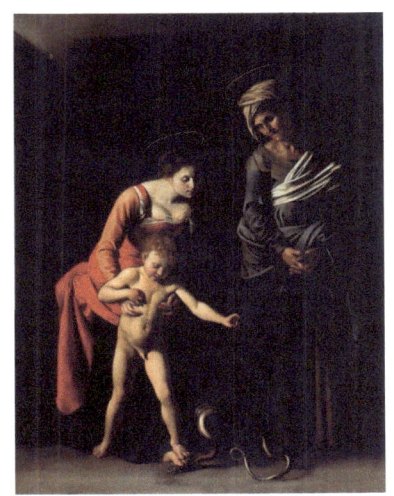
VIRGEN DE LOS PALAFRENEROS

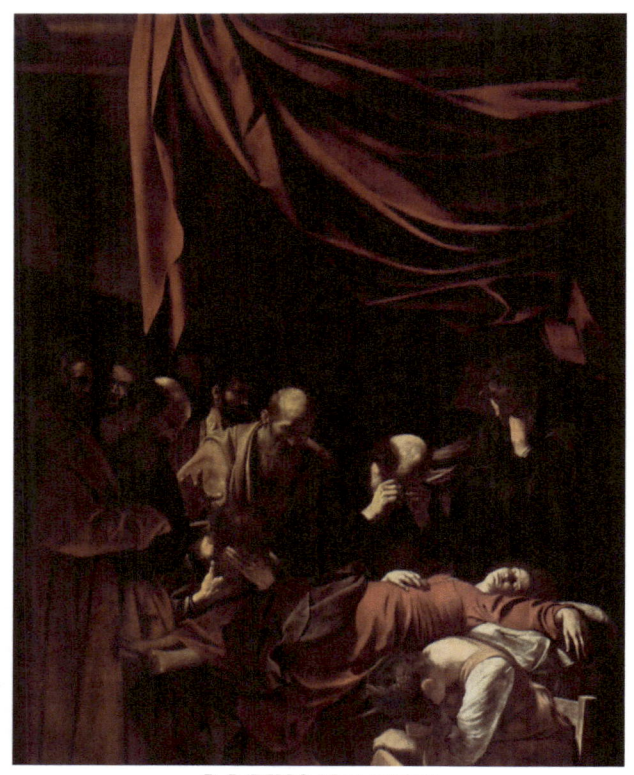

EL ENTIERRO DE LA VIRGEN

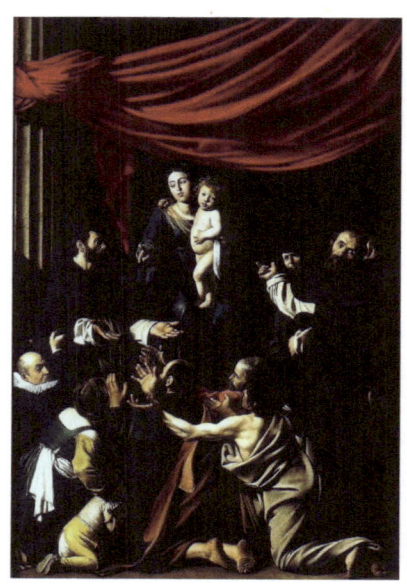

VIRGEN DEL ROSARIO

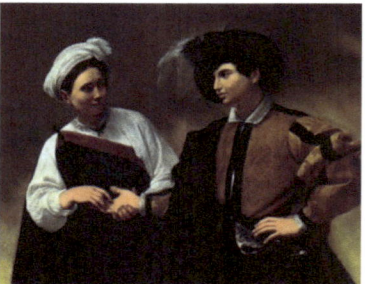
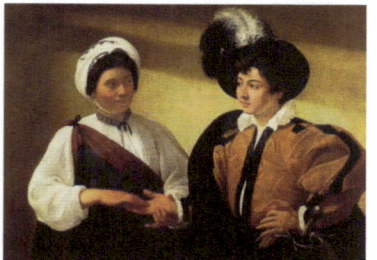

LA BUENAVENTURA I Y II

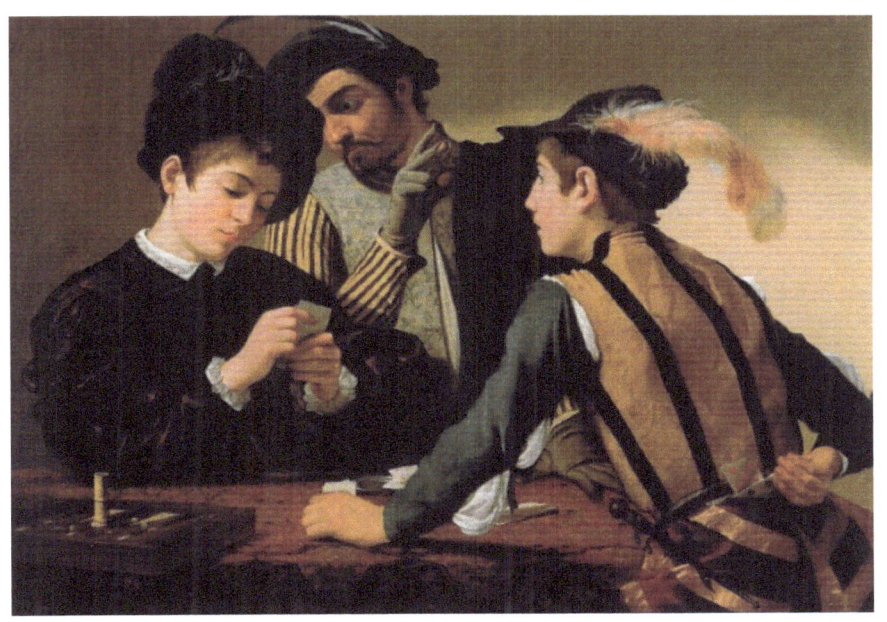

PARTIDA DE CARTAS

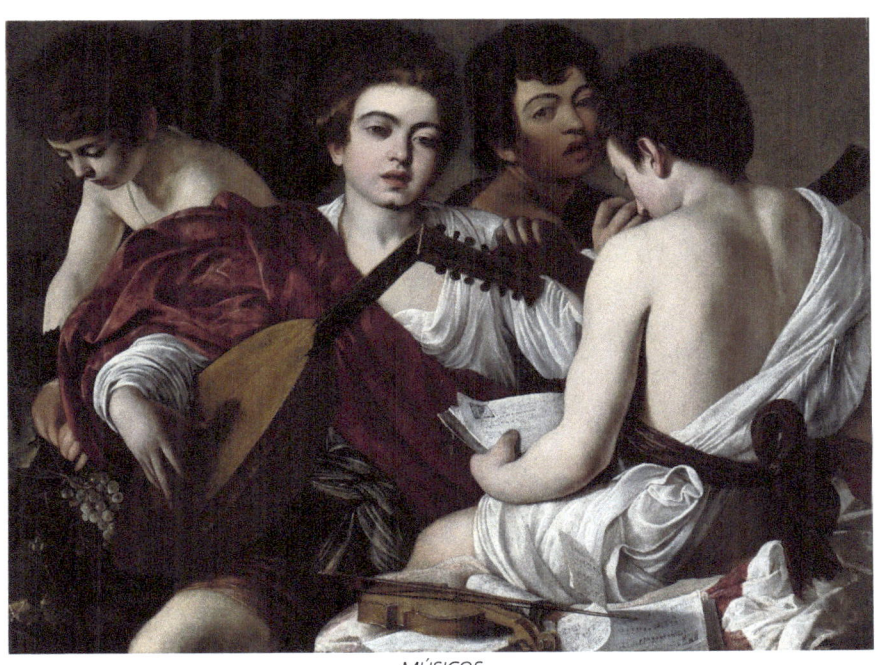

MÚSICOS

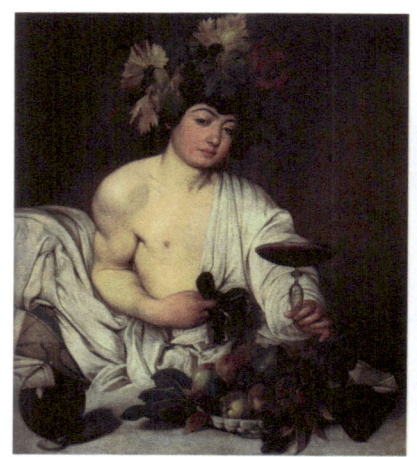
BACO

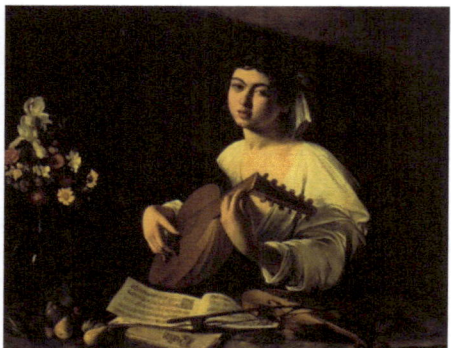
LAUDISTA I

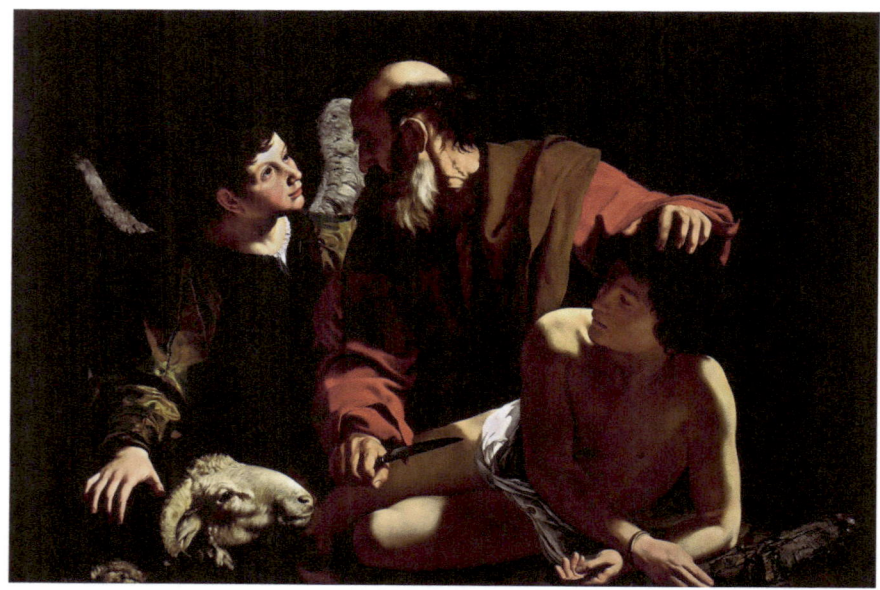
SACRIFICIO DE ISAAC I

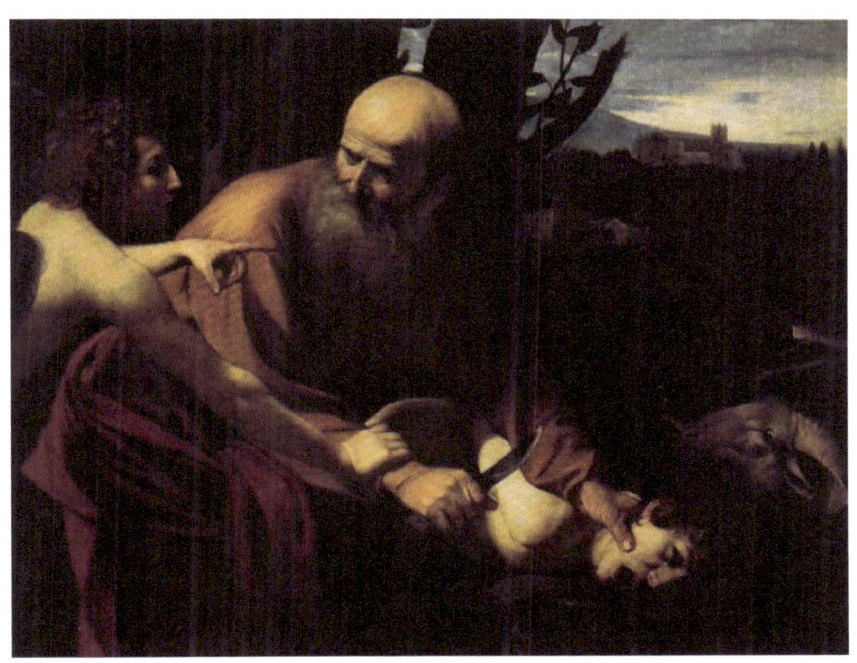

SACRIFICIO DE ISAAC II

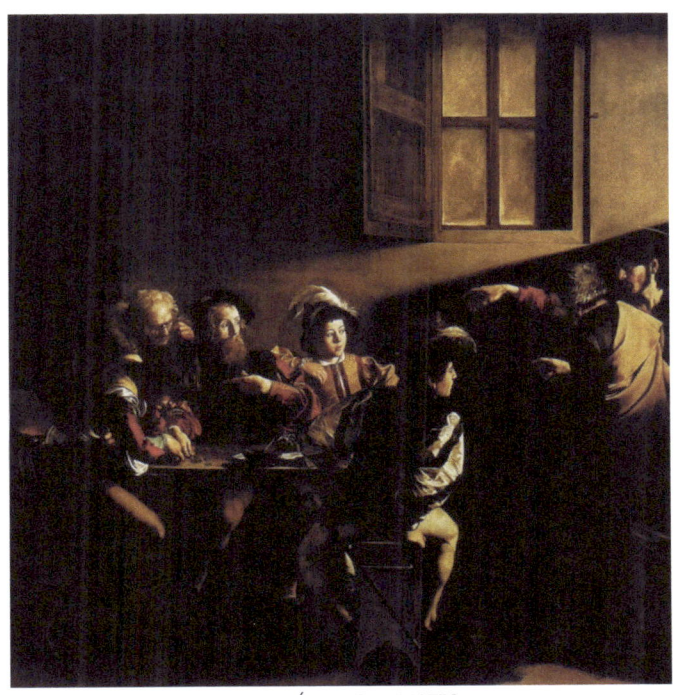

VOCACIÓN DE SAN MATEO

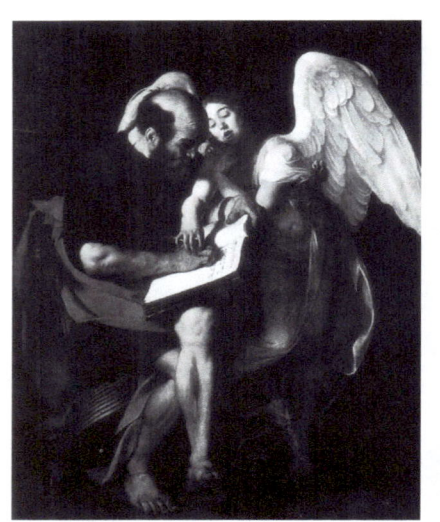
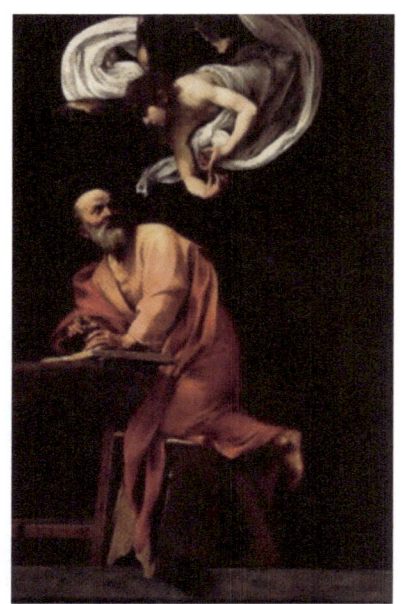

SAN MATEO Y EL ÀNGEL

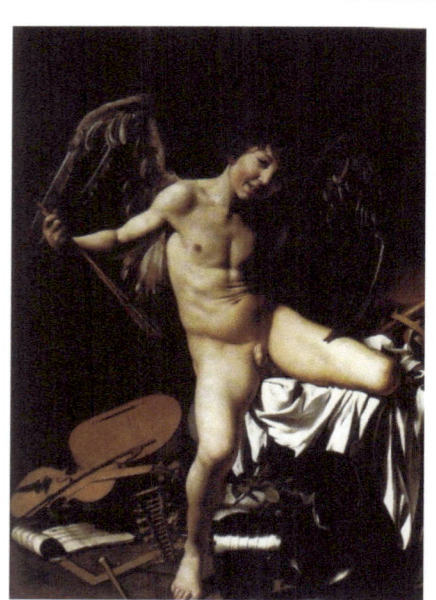

AMOR VICTORIOSO

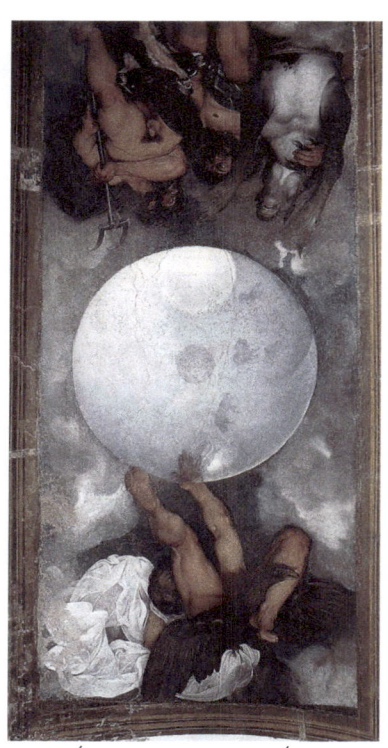

JÚPITER, NEPTUNO, PLUTÓN

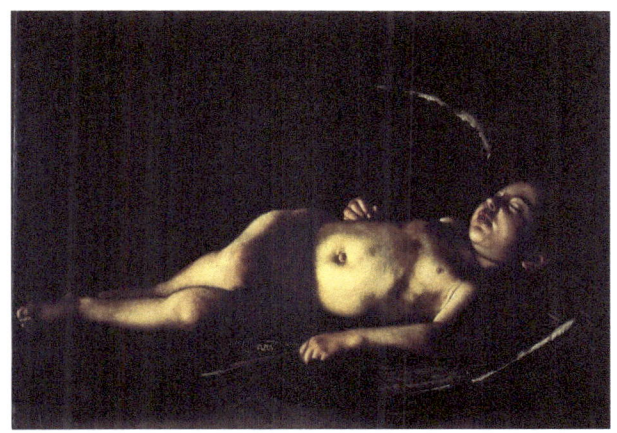

CUPIDO DORMIDO

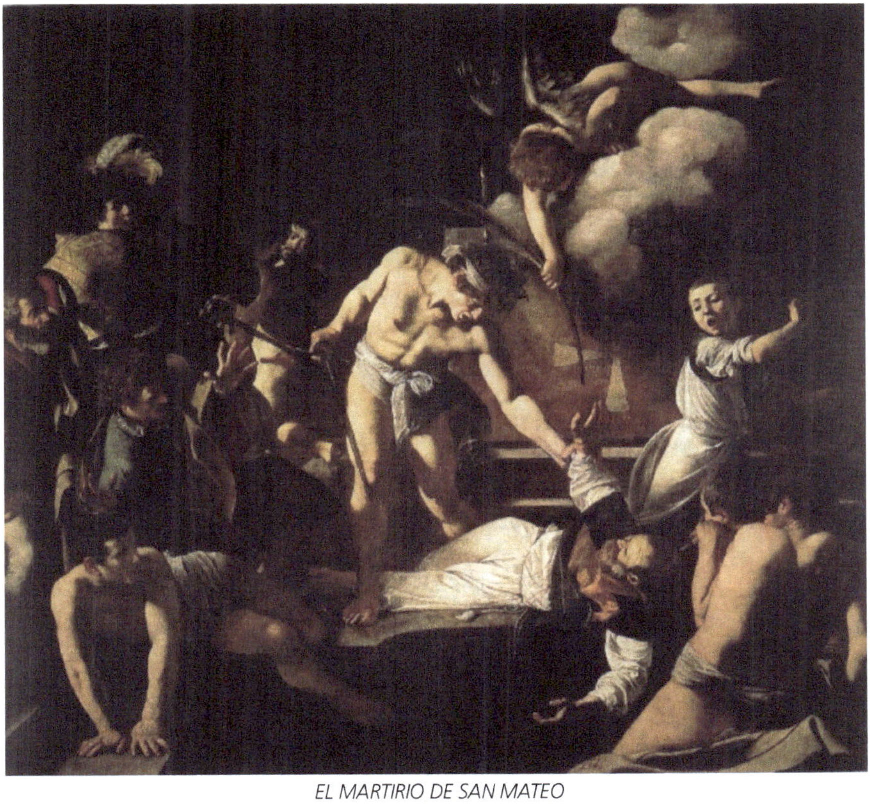

EL MARTIRIO DE SAN MATEO

LIBRO SEGUNDO

Galería

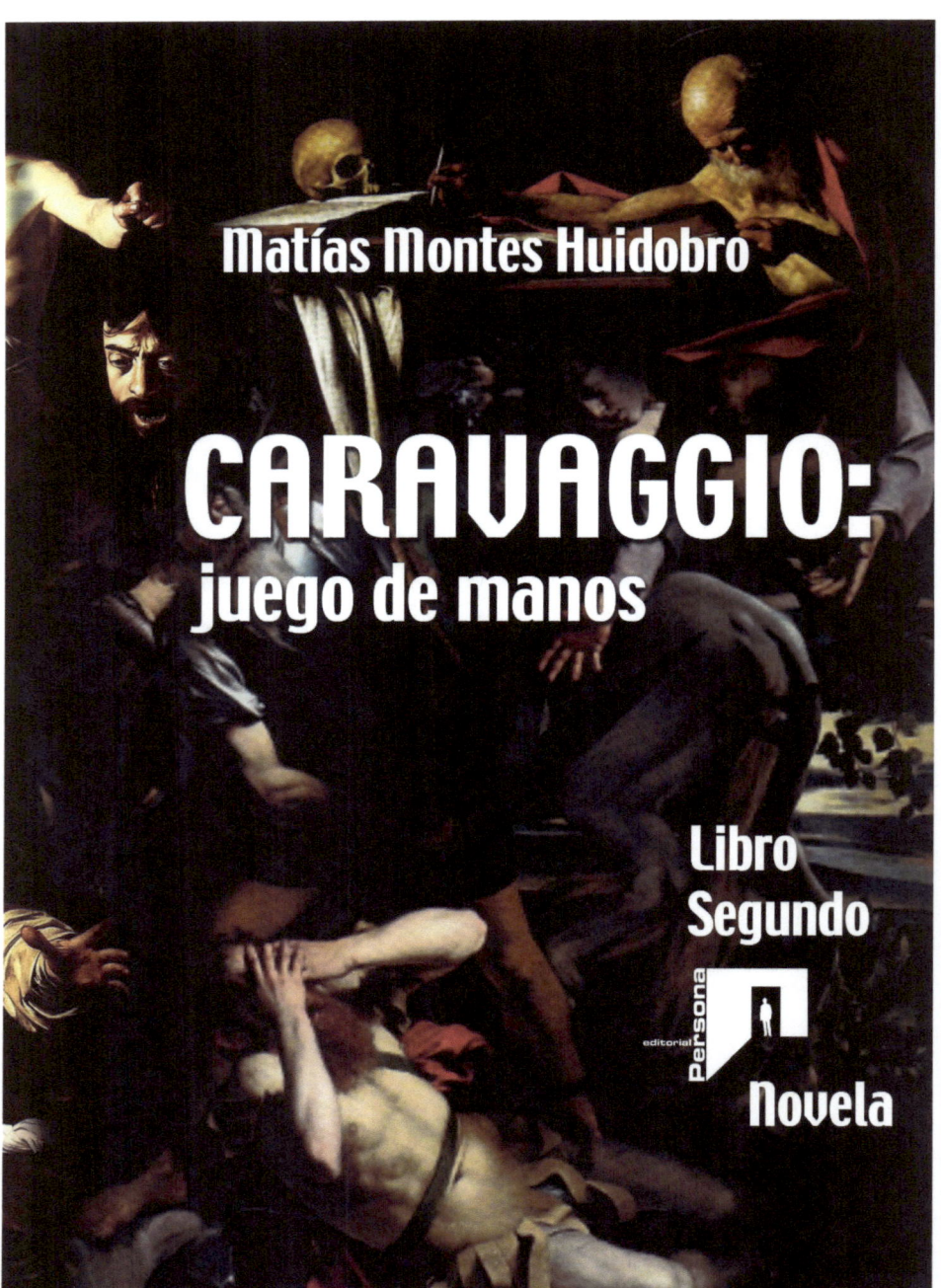

Portada y contra portada: Diseño de Luis García Fresquet

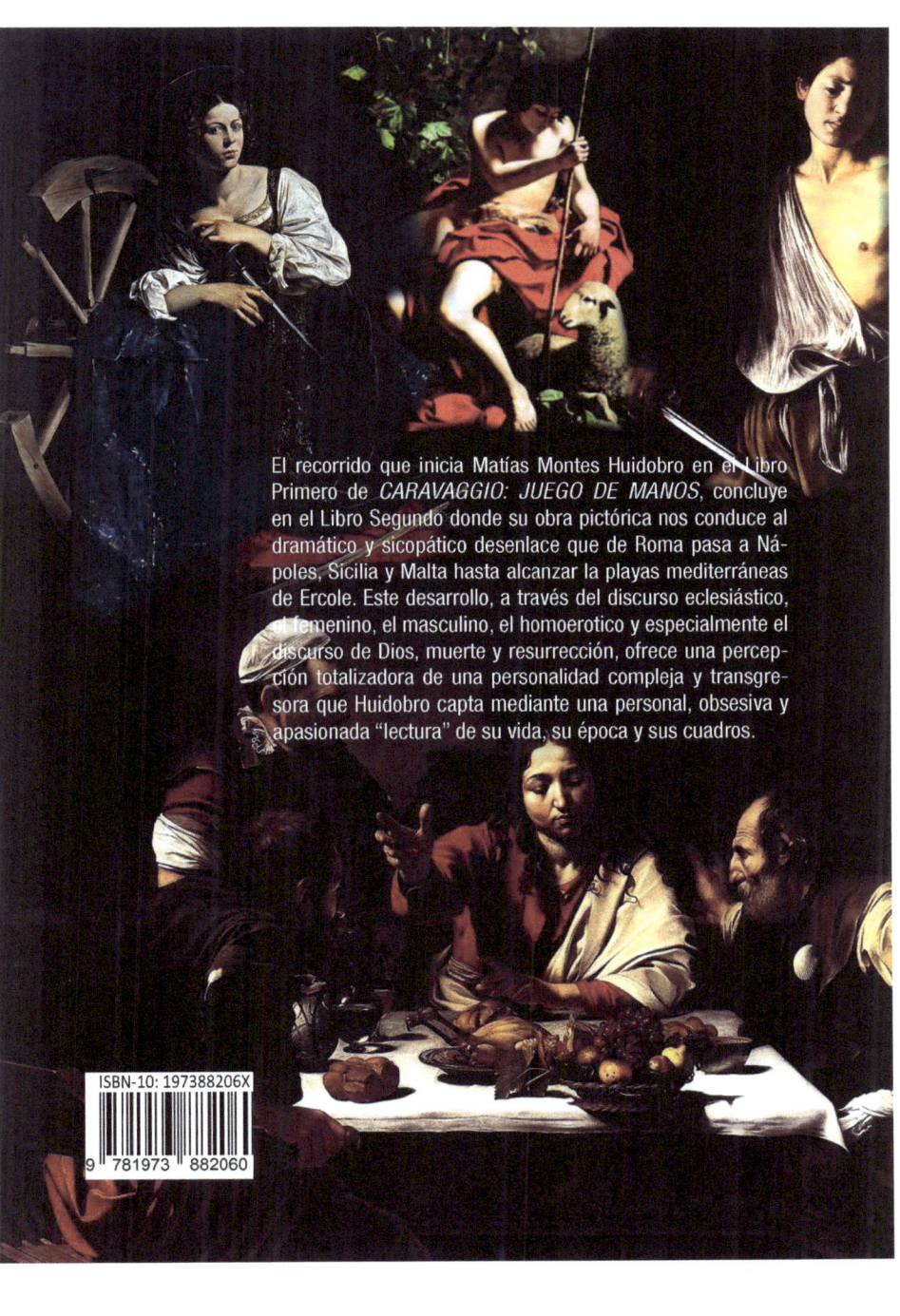

El recorrido que inicia Matías Montes Huidobro en el Libro Primero de *CARAVAGGIO: JUEGO DE MANOS*, concluye en el Libro Segundo donde su obra pictórica nos conduce al dramático y sicopático desenlace que de Roma pasa a Nápoles, Sicilia y Malta hasta alcanzar la playas mediterráneas de Ercole. Este desarrollo, a través del discurso eclesiástico, el femenino, el masculino, el homoerotico y especialmente el discurso de Dios, muerte y resurrección, ofrece una percepción totalizadora de una personalidad compleja y transgresora que Huidobro capta mediante una personal, obsesiva y apasionada "lectura" de su vida, su época y sus cuadros.

ISBN-10: 197388206X

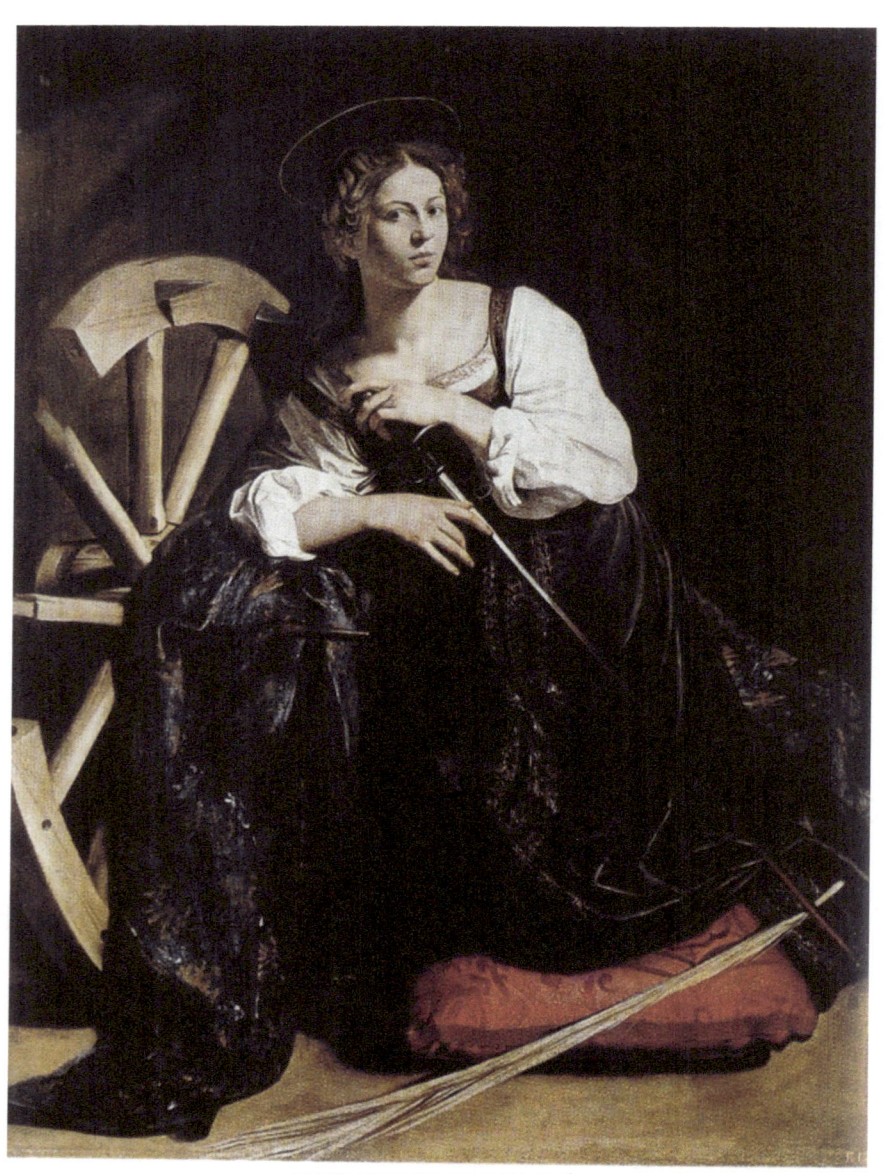

SANTA CATALINA DE ALEJANDRÍA

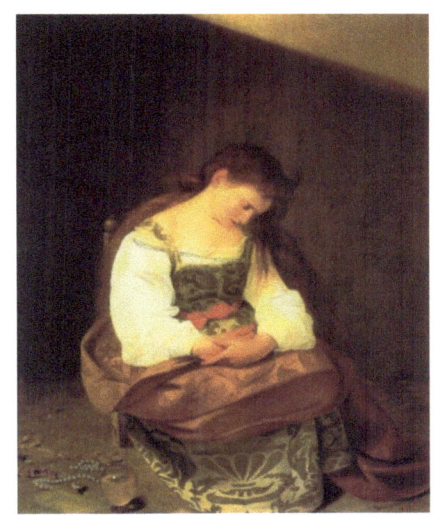
MAGDALENA PENITENTE

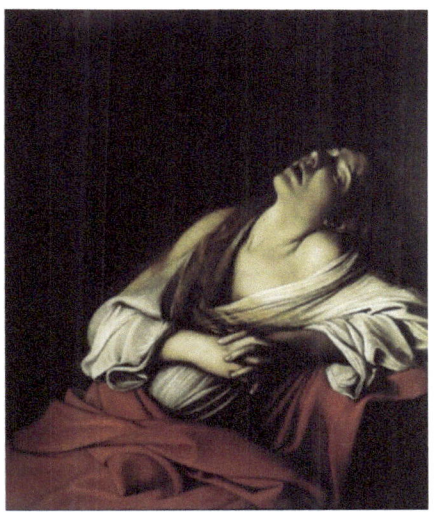
MAGDALENA EN ÉXTASIS

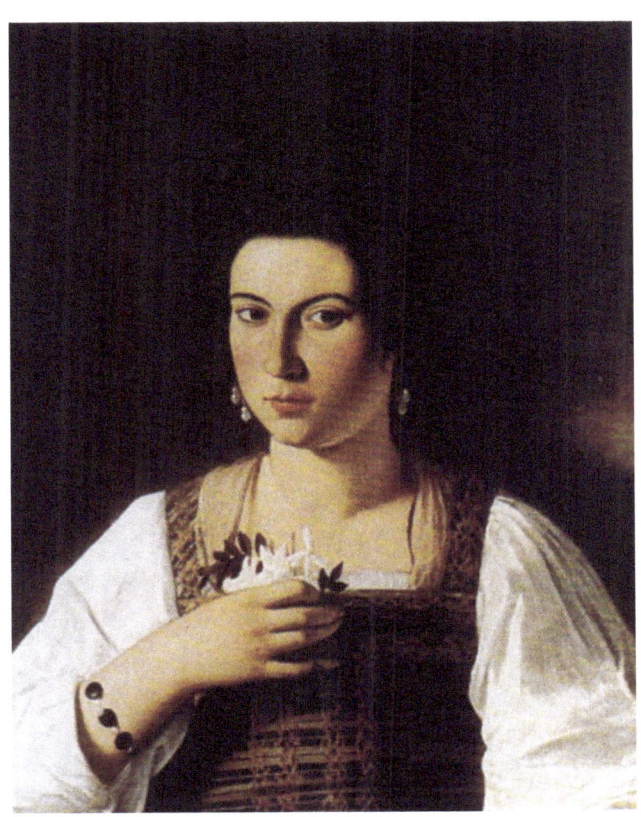
FILIS MELANDRONI

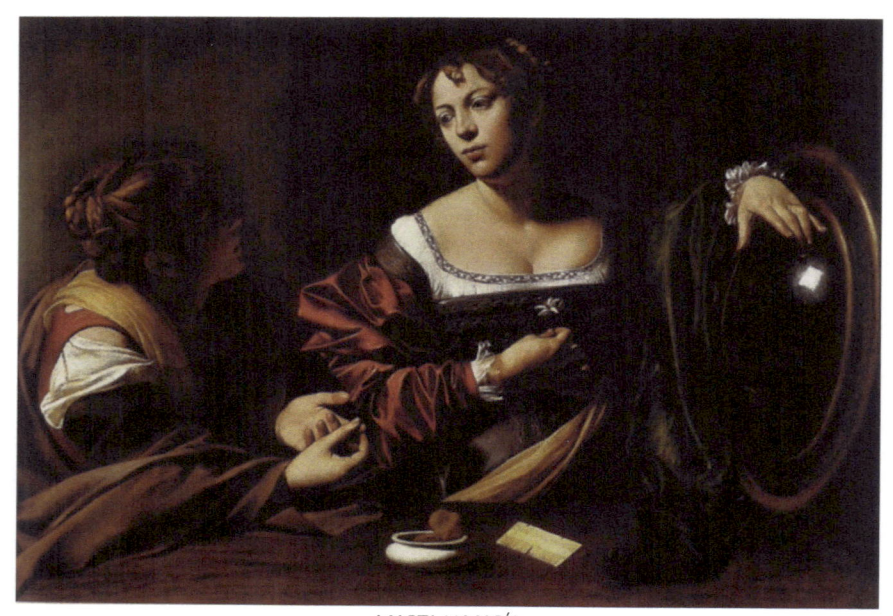

MARTA Y MARÍA

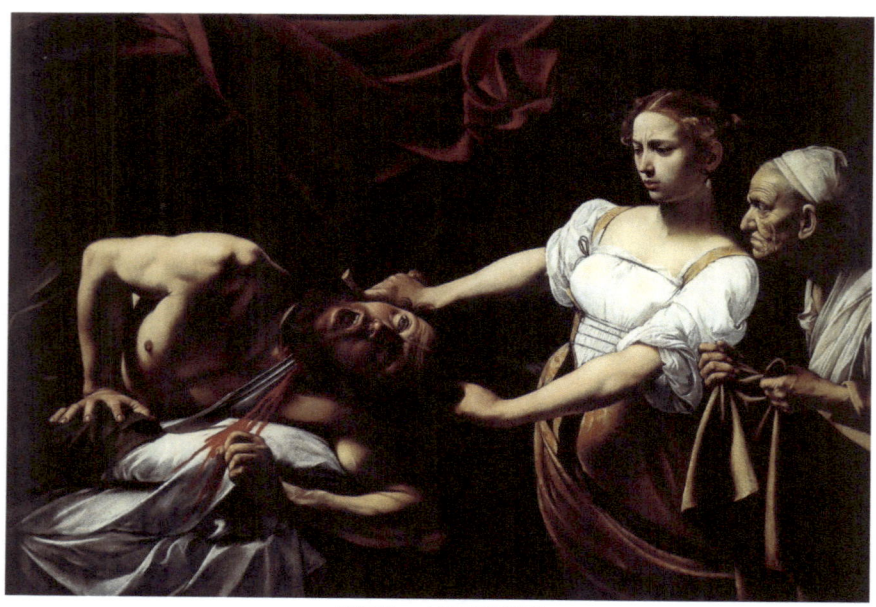

JUDITH y HOLOFERNES

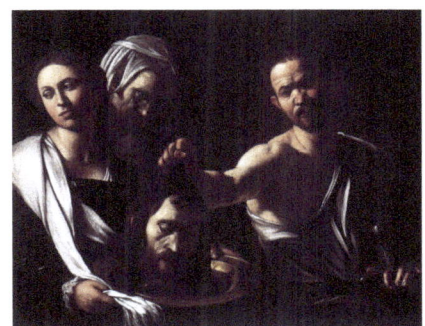 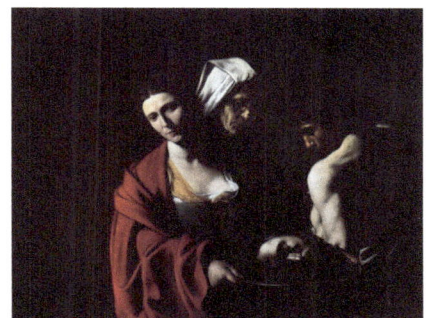

SALOMÉ CON LA CABEZA DE SAN JUAN I y II

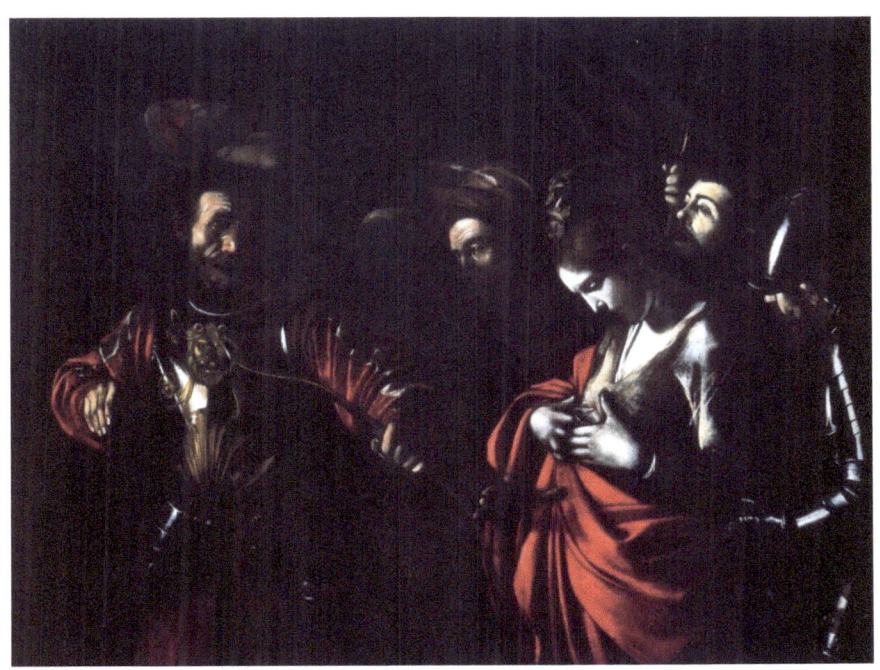

MARTIRIO DE SANTA ÚRSULA

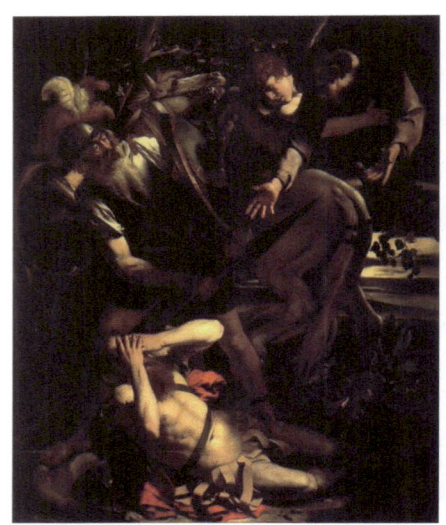
CONVERSIÓN DE SAN PABLO I

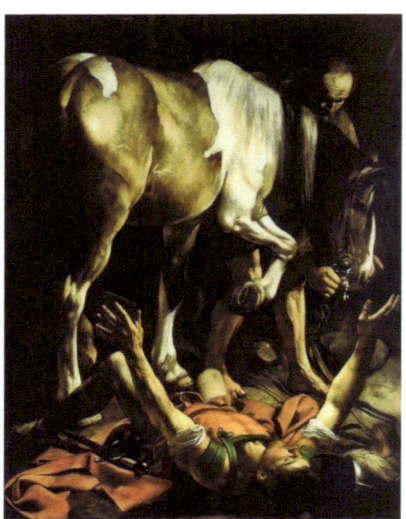
CONVERSIÓN DE SAN PABLO II

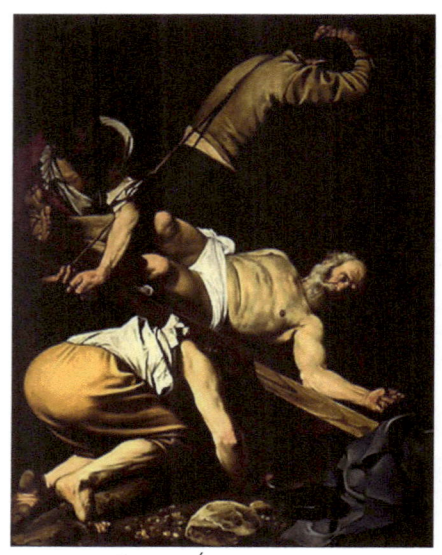
CRUCIFIXIÓN DE SAN PEDRO

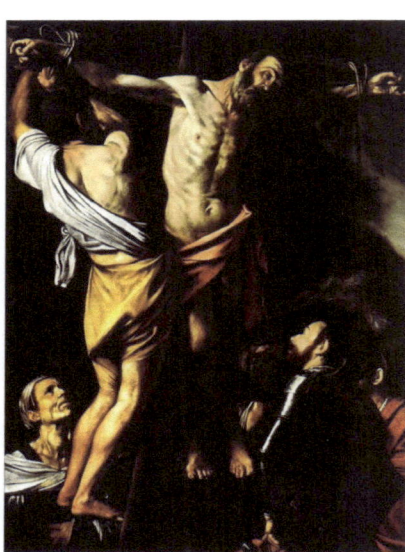
CRUCIFIXIÓN DE SAN ANDRÉS

SAN JERÓNIMO

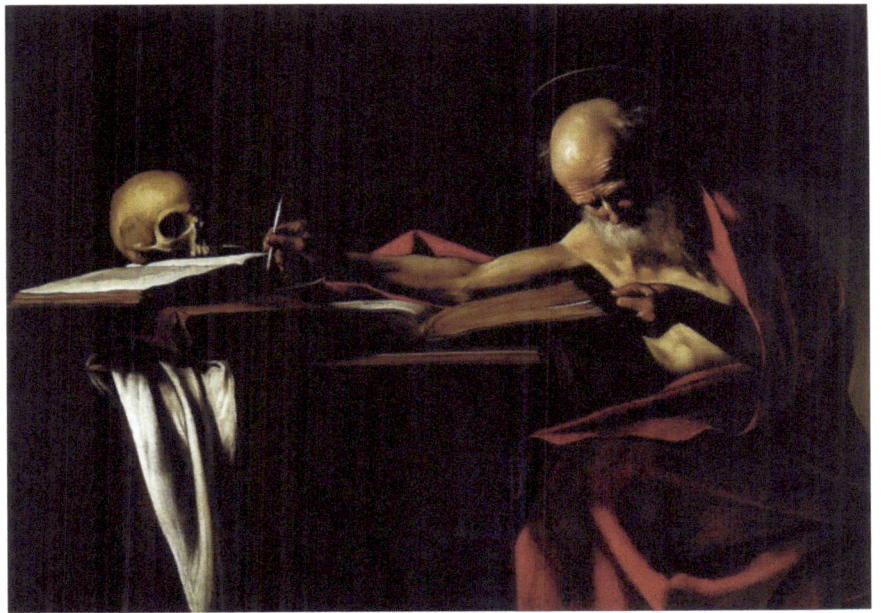

ESCRIBIENDO

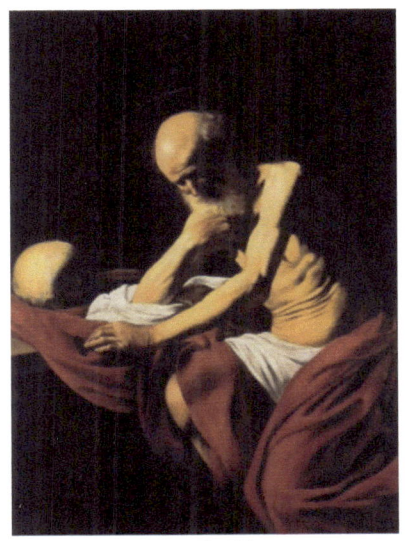

MEDITANDO

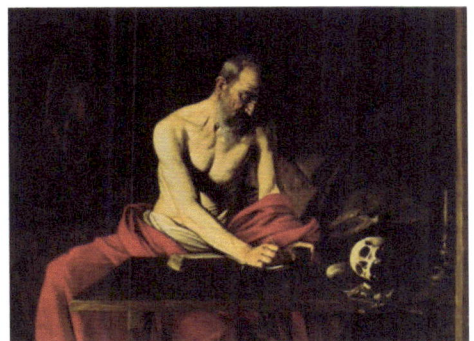

ESCRIBIENDO

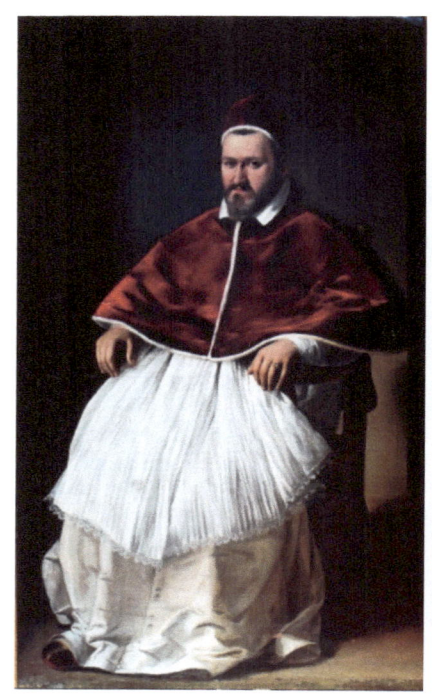
PABLO V BORGHESE

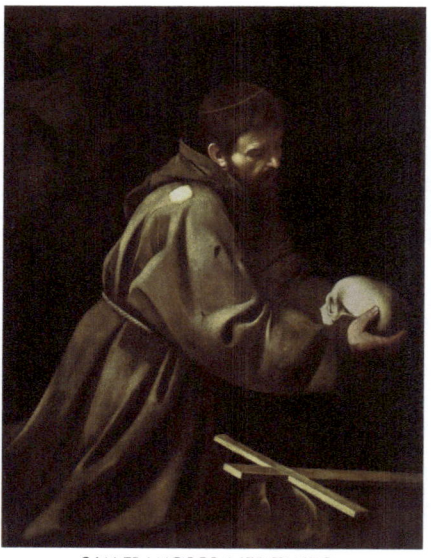
SAN FRANCISCO MEDITANDO

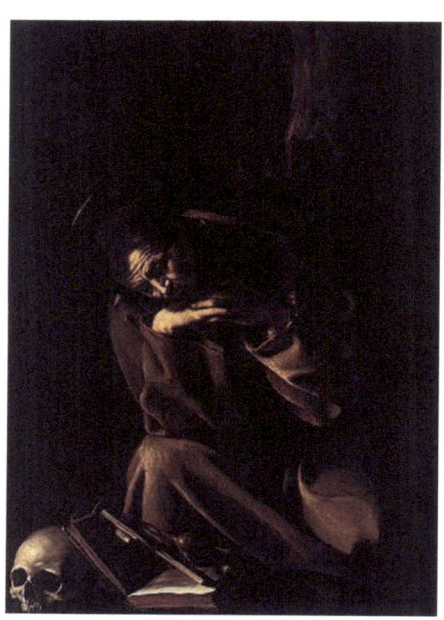
SAN FRANCISCO PENITENTE

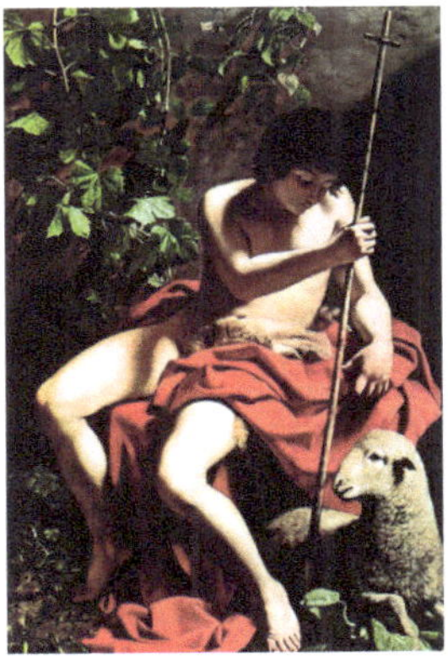

SAN JUAN BAUTISTA

1598

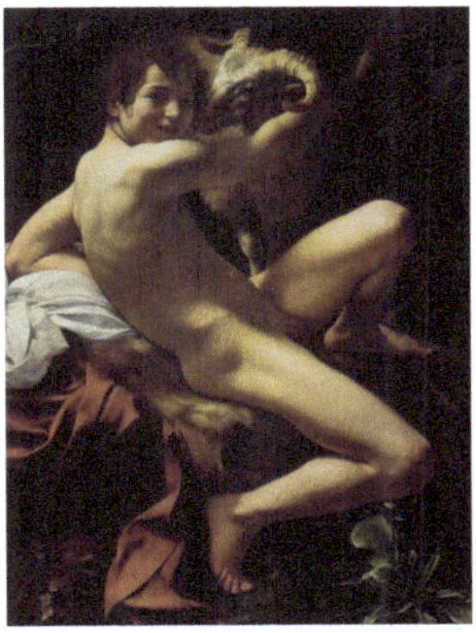

1602

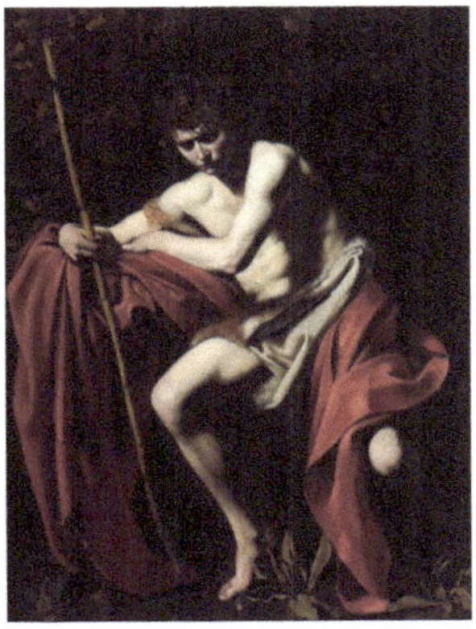

1602

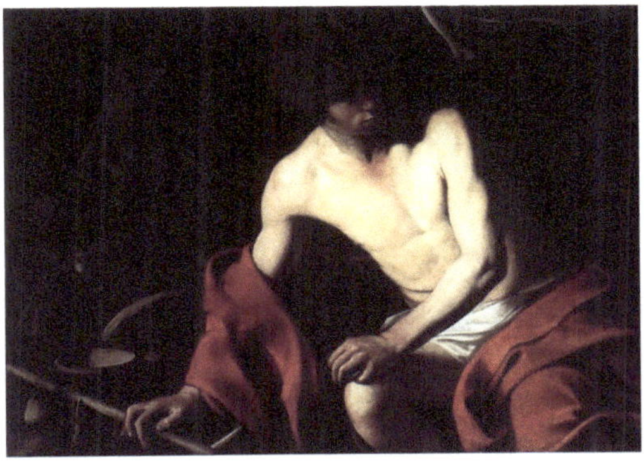

1603

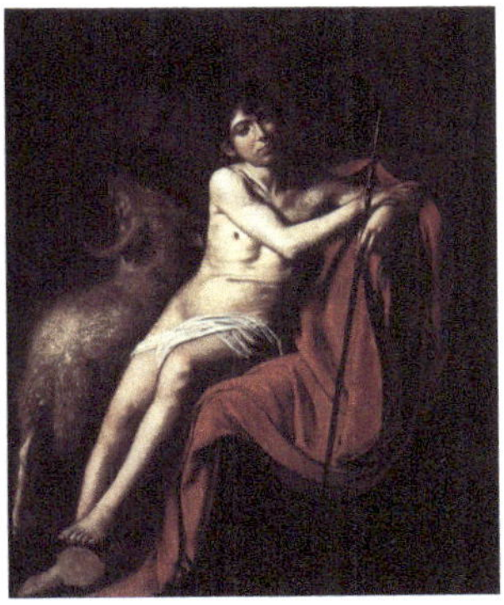

1610

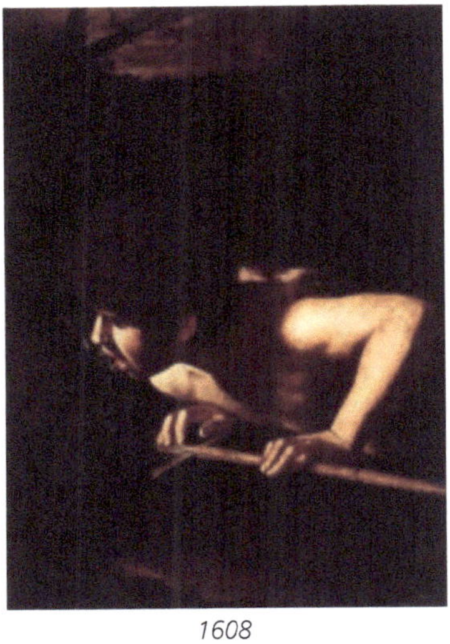

1608

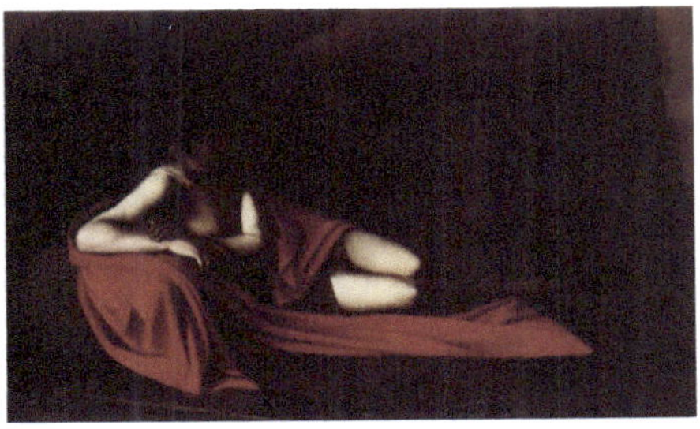

1610

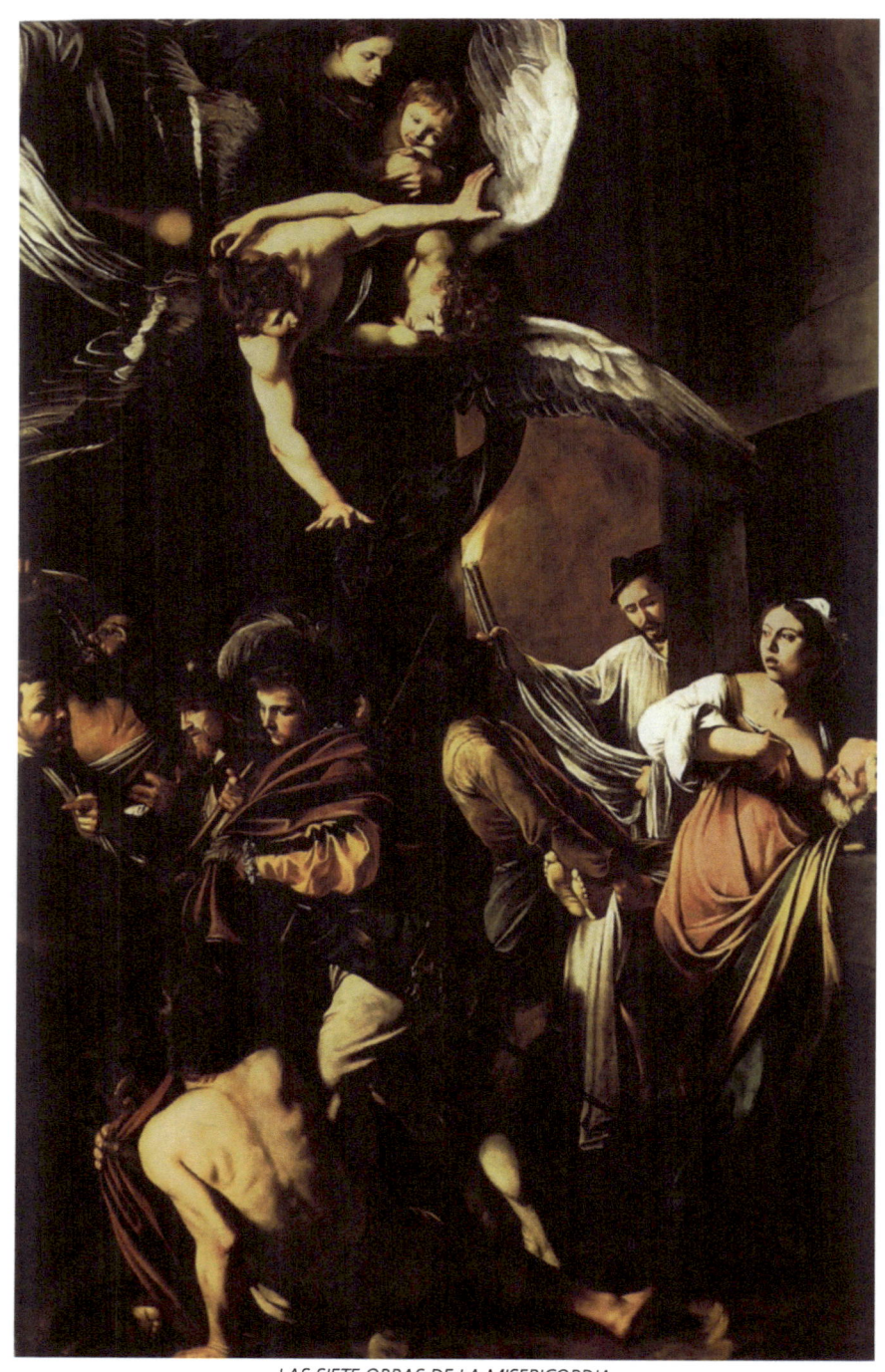

LAS SIETE OBRAS DE LA MISERICORDIA

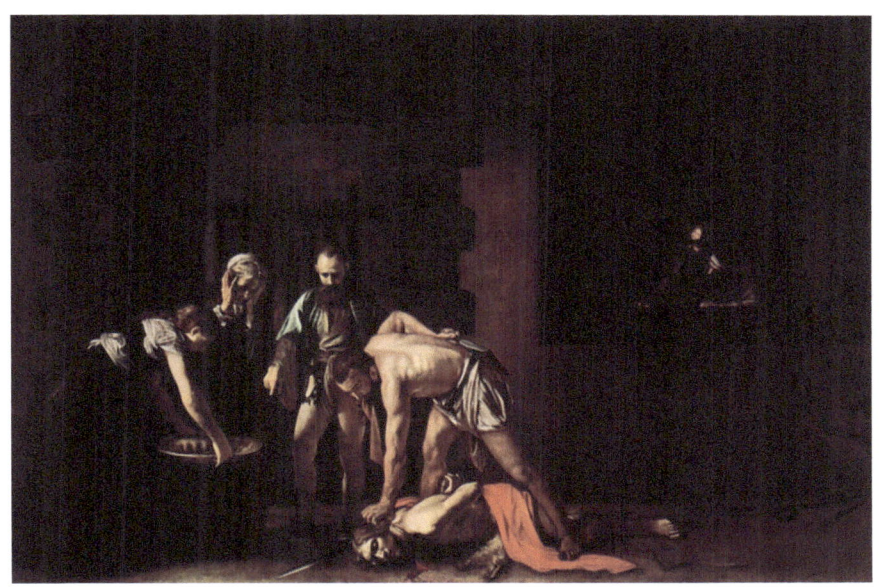
DESCAPITACIÓN DE SAN JUAN BAUTISTA

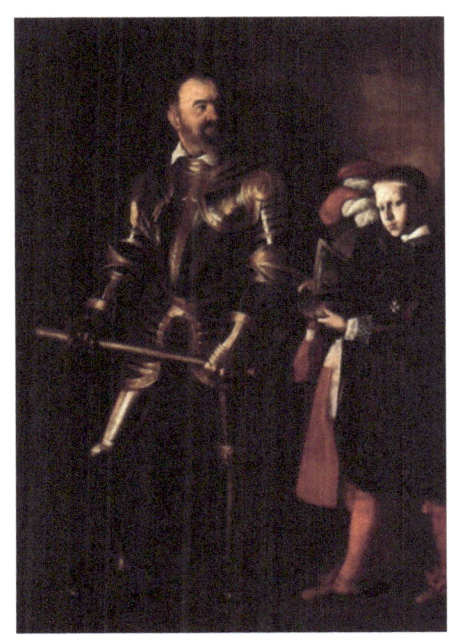
ALOF DE WIGNACOURT

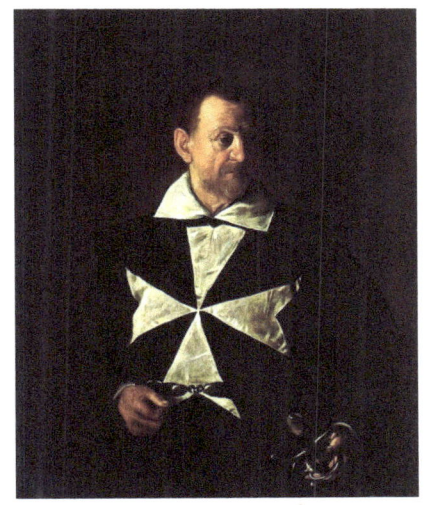
ANTONIO MARTINELLI

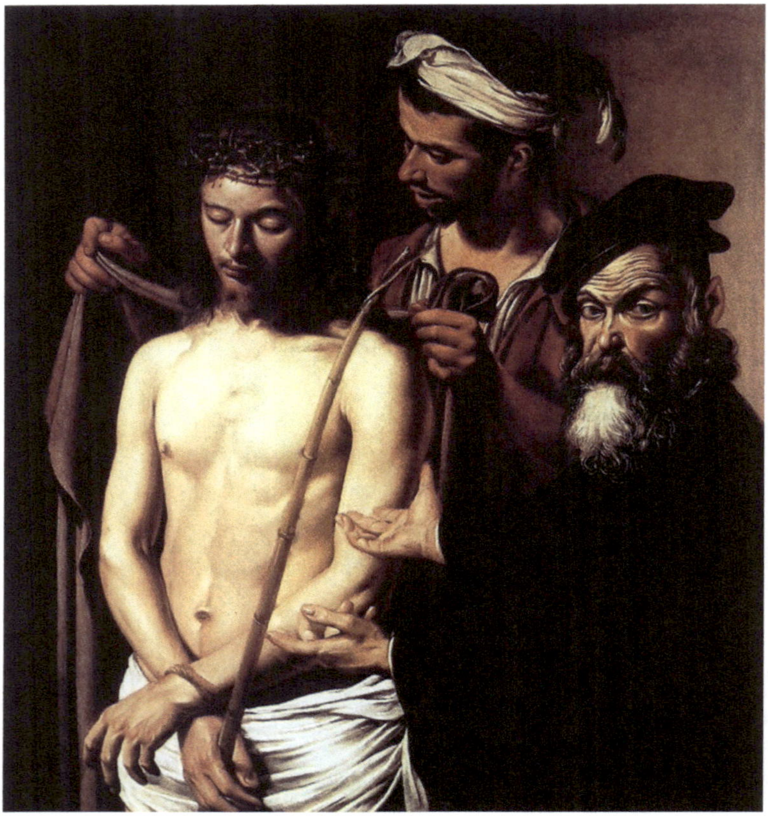

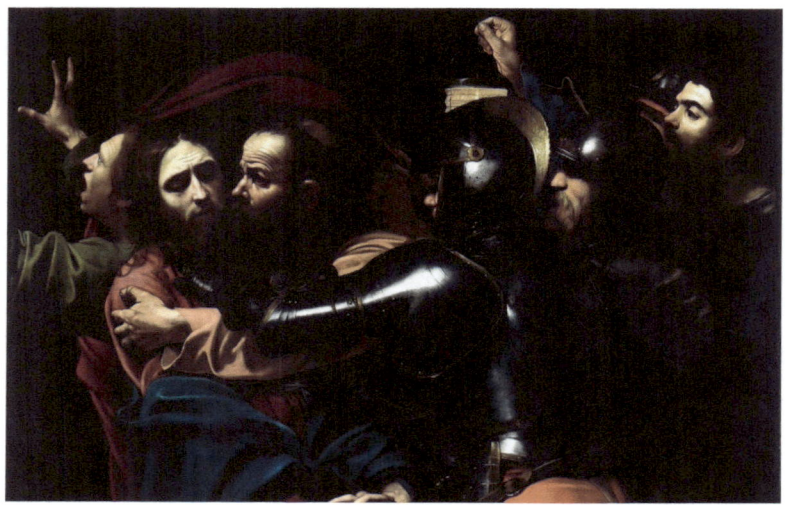

ECCE HOMO

PRENDICIÓN DE CRISTO

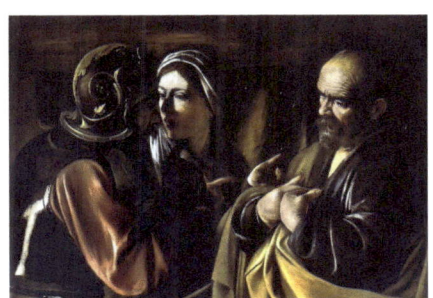
NEGACIÓN DE SAN PEDRO

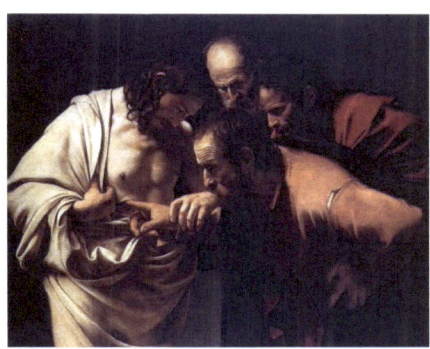
INCREDULIDAD DE SANTO TOMÁS

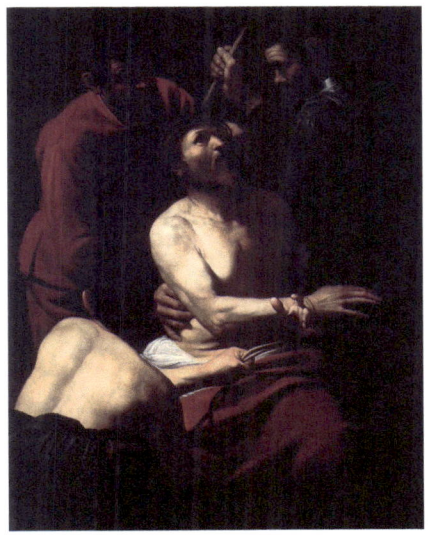
CORONA DE ESPINAS I

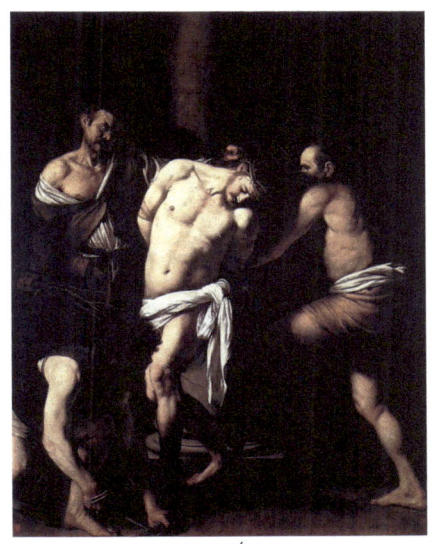
FLAGELACIÓN I

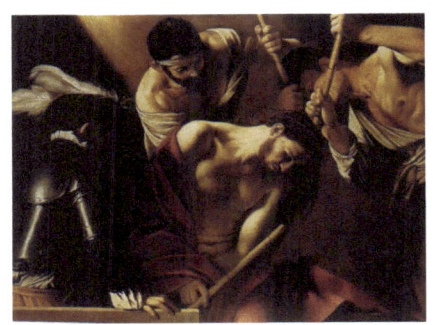
CORONA DE ESPINAS II

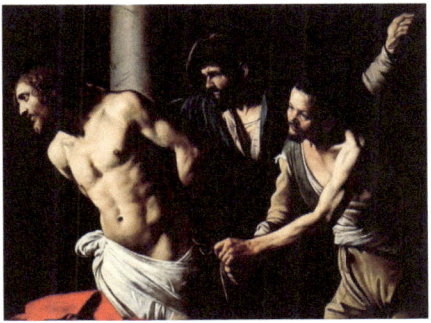
FLAGELACION II

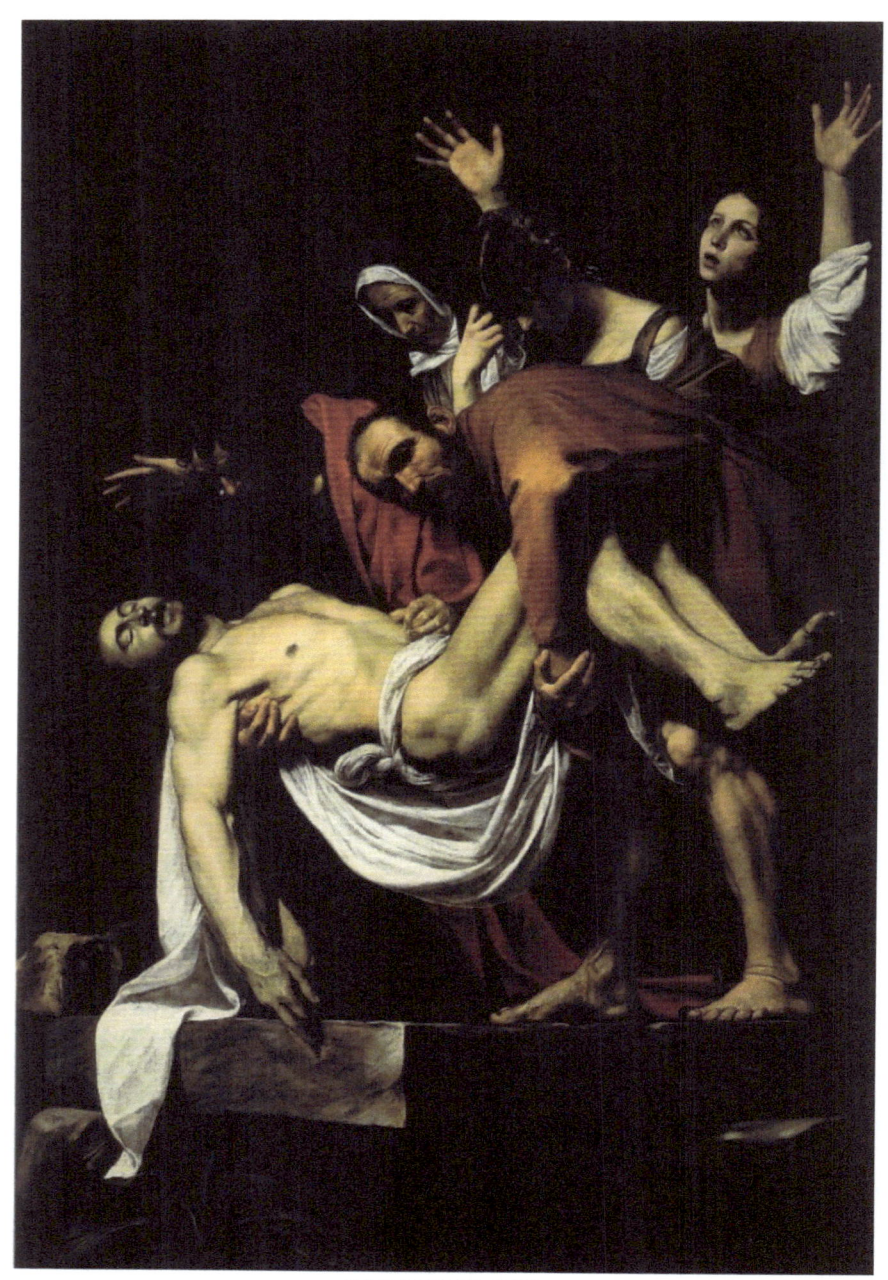

EL ENTIERRO DE CRISTO

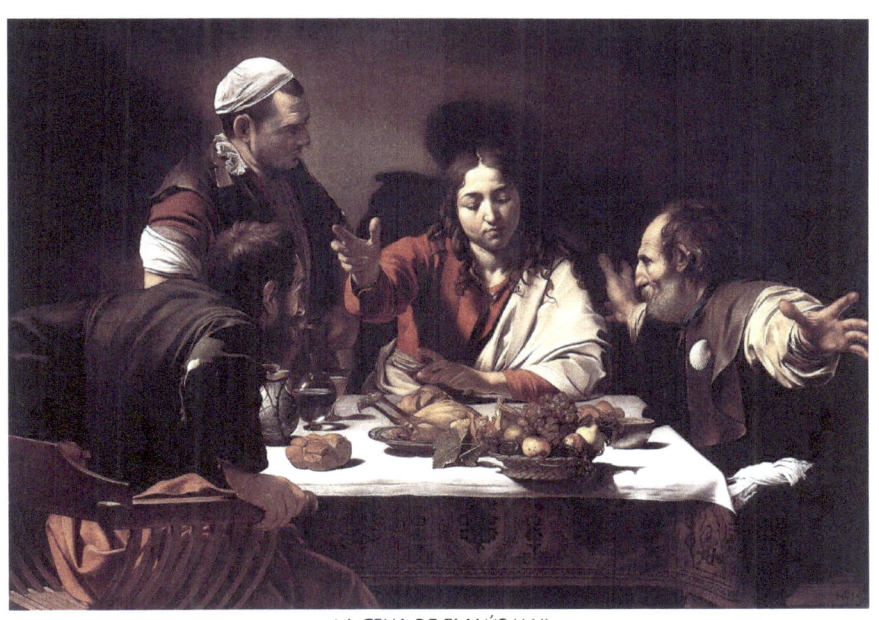

LA CENA DE EMAÚS I Y II

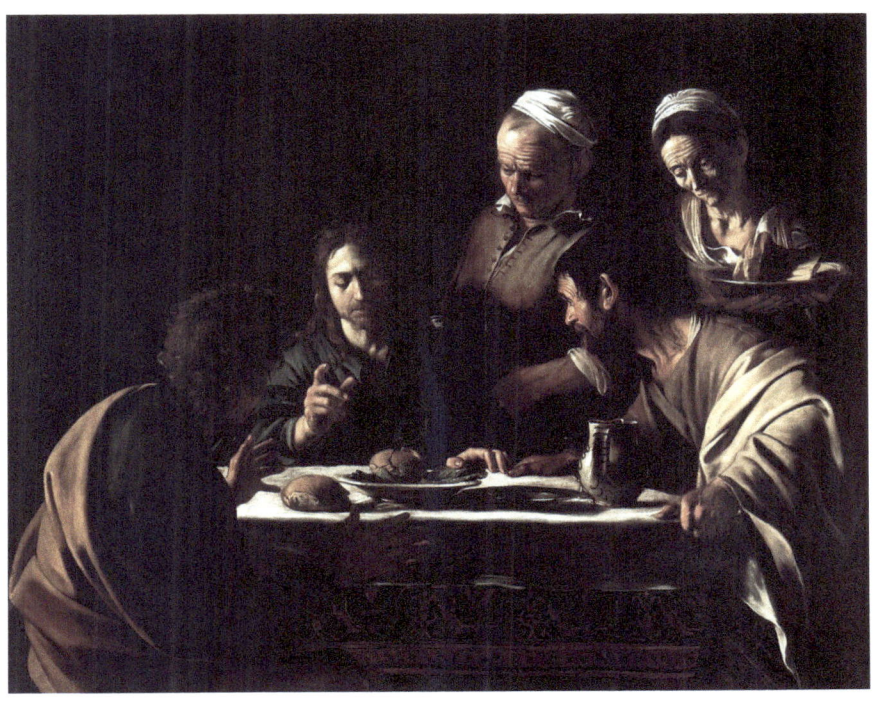

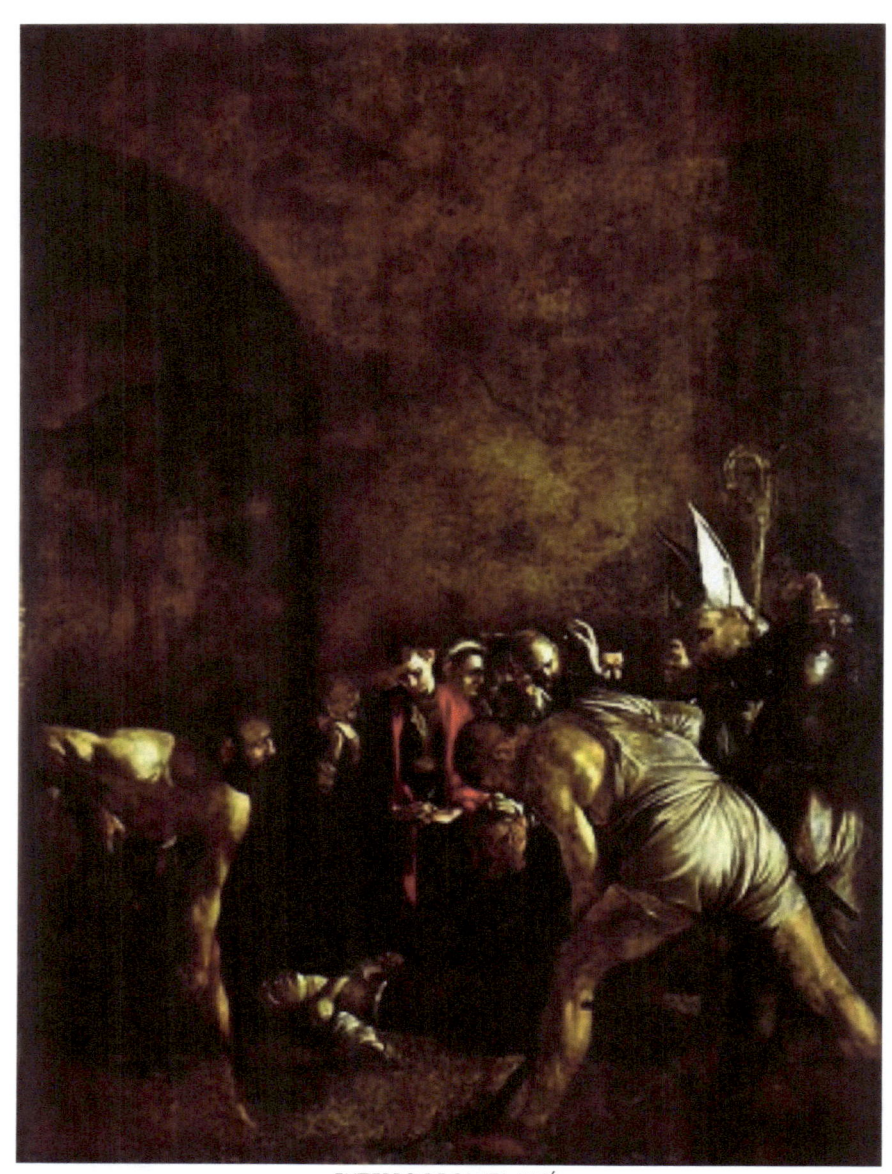

ENTIERRO DE SANTA LUCÍA

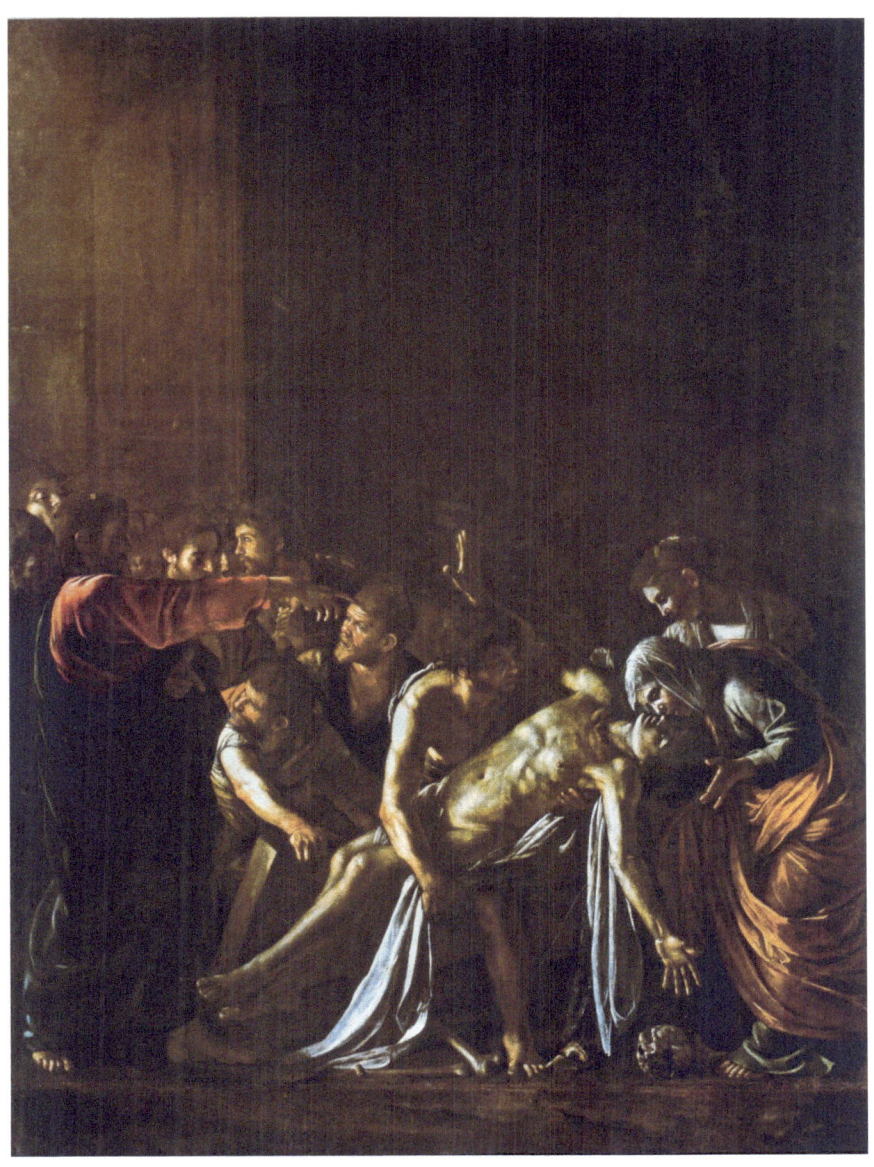

RESURRECCIÓN DE LÁZARO

DAVID CON LA CABEZA DE GOLIAT

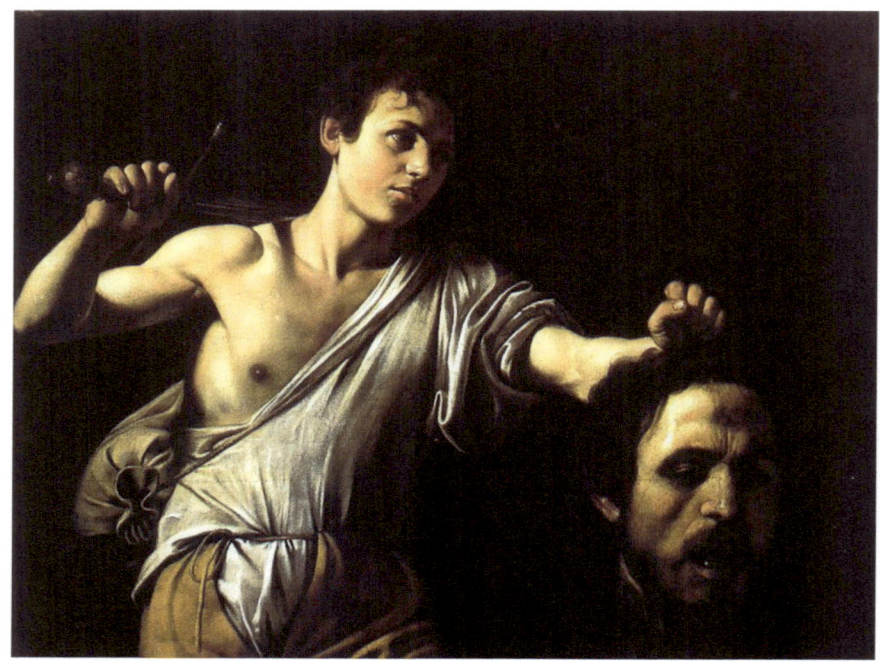

1599

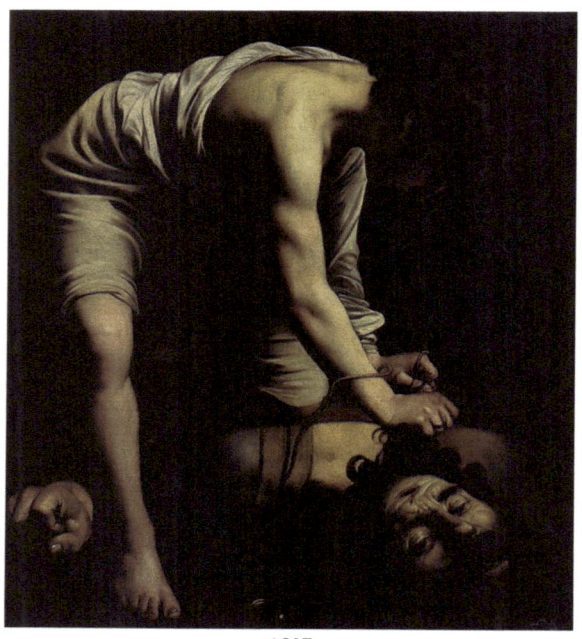

1607

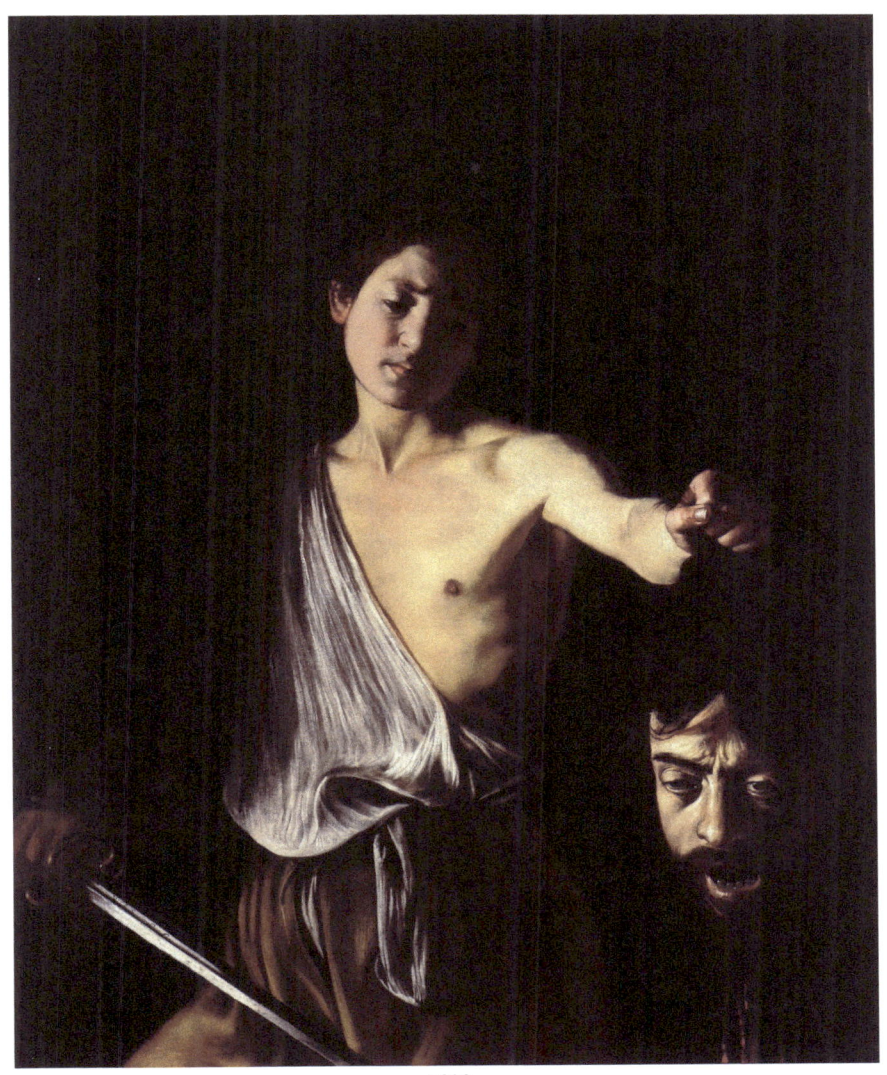

1606

ITINERARIO PICTÓRICO: OBRAS DISCUTIDAS

Muchacho pelando un bergamoto (1593)	Roma	Colección privada
Baco enfermo (1593)	Roma	Galería Borghese
Muchacho con cesta de frutas (1593)	Roma	Galería Borghese
La buenaventura I (1594)	Roma	Museo Capitolino
Partida de cartas (1595)	Fort Worth	Art Museum Kimbell
La buenaventura II (1595)	París	Museo del Louvre
Músicos (1595)	New York	Metropolitan Museum
El éxtasis de San Francisco (1595)	Hartford	Ateneo Wadsford
Muchacho mordido por un lagarto (1596)	Florencia	Fundación Roberto Longhi
Laudista I (1596)	S. Petersburgo	Museo del Ermitage
Laudista II (1596)	New York	Metropolitan Museum
Baco (1596)	Florencia	Galería Uffizi
Magdalena penitente (1597)	Roma	Galería Doria Pamphilj
Descanso de la huida a Egipto (1597)	Roma	Galerìa Doria Pamphilj
Cabeza de Medusa (1597)	Florencia	Galería Uffizi
Retrato de Filis Melandroni (1597)	Berlín	Friederich Museum
Júpiter, Neptuno, Plutón (1597)	Roma	Casino della Villa Ludovisi
Santa Catalina de Alejandría (1598)	Madrid	Museum Thyssen Bornemisza
Sacrificio de Isaac I (1598)	Princenton	Colección Barbara P. Johnson
San Juan Bautista I (1598)	Toledo	Museo de la Catedral
Marta y Magdalena (1598)	Detroit	Detroit Institute of Art
Cesta de frutas (1599)	Milán	Pinacoteca Ambrosiana
Judith y Holofernes (1599)	Roma	Galería Nacional, Palacio Barberini
David con la cabeza de Goliat I (1599)	Madrid	Museo del Prado
Narciso (1599)	Roma	Galería Nacional, Palacio Corsini
La vocación de San Mateo (1599-1600)	Roma	Iglesia de San Luigi dei Francesi
El martirio de San Mateo (1599-1600)	Roma	Iglesia de San Luigi dei Francesi
Conversión de San Pablo I (1601)	Roma	Colección Odescalchi

Conversión de San Pablo II (1601)	Roma	Iglesia Santa María del Popolo
Crucifixión de San Pedro (1601)	Roma	Iglesia Santa María del Popolo
La cena de Emaús I (1601)	Londres	National Gallery
Amor victorioso (1602)	Berlín	Gemaldegalerie
San Mateo y el ángel I (1602)	Berlín	Destruido en 1945
San Mateo y el ángel II (1602)	Roma	Iglesia de San Luigi dei Francese
San Juan Bautista II (1602)	Roma	Museo Capitolino, Pinacoteca
San Juan Bautista III (1602)	Roma	Galería Doria Pamphilj
La incredulidad de Santo Tomás (1602)	Postdam	Sanssouci Galería de Pintura
El prendimiento de Cristo (1602)	Dublin	National Gallery
El entierro de Cristo (1603)	Roma	Pinacoteca Vaticana
Sacrificio de Isaac II (1603)	Florencia	Galería Uffizi
Virgen de los peregrinos (1604)	Roma	Iglesia de San Agustín
San Juan Bautista IV (1604)	Kansas City	Atkins Museum
San Juan Bautista V (1604)	Roma	Galería Nacional, Palacio Corsini
Coronación de espinas I (1604)	Prato	Caja de Ahorros y Depósitos
Muerte de la Virgen (1604)	París	Museo del Louvre
Ecce Homo (1605)	Génova	Galería Palacio Rosso
San Jerónimo escribiendo I (1605)		Montserrat Monasterio de Santa María
San Jerónimo escribiendo II (1605)	Roma	Galería Borghese
Retrato de Pablo V (1605)	Roma	Galería Borghese
Virgen de los palafreneros (1606)	Roma	Galería Borghese
Magdalena en éxtasis (1606)	Roma	Colección privada
La cena de Emaús II (1606)	Milán	Pinacoteca de Brera
David con la cabeza de Goliat II (1606)	Roma	Galería Borghese
San Francisco penitente I (1606)	Cremona	Pinacoteca de la ciudad
San Francisco penitente II (1606)	Roma	Museo del Palacio Venecia
Siete obras de la misericordia (1606)	Nápoles	Iglesia Pio Monte de la Misericordia
Crucifixión de San Andrés (1607)	Cleveland	Cleveland Museum of Art
David con la cabeza de Goliat III (1607)	Viena	Kunsthistorisches Museum
Virgen del Rosario (1607)	Viena	Kunsthistorisches Museum

Coronación de espinas II (1607)	Viena	Kunsthistorisches Museum
Flagelación de Cristo I (1607)	Nápoles	Museo Nacional Campodimonte
Flagelación de Cristo II (1607)	Ruán	Museo de Bellas Artes
Salomé con la cabeza de San Juan I (1607)	Londres	National Gallery
San Jerónimo escribiendo III (1608)	Valletta	Museo Co-Catedral de San Juan
Resurrección de Cristo (1608)	Berlín	Destruido en 1945
Retrato de Alof de Wignacourt (1608)	Paris	Museo del Louvre
Antonio Martelli (1608)	Florencia	Palacio Pitti, Galería Palatina
Decapitación de San Juan Bautista (1608)	Valletta	Museo Co-Catedral de San Juan
Amor dormido (1608)	Florencia	Palacio Pitti, Galería Palatina
San Juan Bautista VI (1608)	Valletta	Colección Bonelli, Malta
Anunciación (1608)	Nancy	Museo de Bellas Artes
Entierro de Santa Lucía (1608)	Siracusa	Museo del Palacio Bellomo
Resurrección de Lázaro (1609)	Messina	Museo Provincial
Natividad I (1609)	Messina	Museo Provincial
Natividad II (1609)	Palermo	Paradero actual desconocido
Salomé con la cabeza de San Juan II (1609)	Nápoles	Galería Nacional Campo di Monti
Negación de San Pedro (1610)	New York	Colección privada
San Juan Bautista (1610)	Roma	Galería Borghese
San Juan Bautista (1610)	Munich	Colección privada
Martirio de Santa Úrsula (1610)	Nápoles	Banca Comercial Italiana

GALERÍAS

ITALIA

ROMA

Galería Borghese
Museo Capitolino
Galería Doria Pamphilj
Casino de la Villa Ludovisi
Galería Nacional de Arte Antiguo Palacio Barberini
Galería Nacional de Arte Antiguo Palacio Corsini
Iglesia San Luigi dei Francesi
Iglesia de San Agustín
Colección Odescalchi
Iglesia Sta. María del Popolo
Pinacoteca Vaticana
Palacio Venecia
Fundación Roberto Longi

NÁPOLES

Iglesia Pio Monte de la Misericordia
Museo Nacional de Campodimonte

SIRACUSA
Palacio Bellomo

MESSINA
Museo Provincial

PALERMO
Compañía San Lorenzo

MILÁN
Pinacoteca Ambrosiana

FIORENCIA
Galería de los Uffizi
Palacio Pitti

GENOVA
Palazo Rosso

PRATO
Caja de Ahorros y Depósitos

CREMONA
Pinacoteca

ITINERARIO EUROPEO

MADRID
Museo del Prado
Thyssen Bornemisza
Palacio Real

PARIS
Museo del Louvre

SAN PETERSBURGO
Museo del Ermitage

LONDRES National Gallery	**VIENA** Kuntsthitorisches	**DUBLIN** National Gallery
TOLEDO Museo de la Catedral	**POSTMAN** Galería Sanssouci	**RUÁN** Museo de Bellas Artes
BERLIN Kaiser Friederich Museum	**NANCY** Bellas Artes	**MONSERRAT** Museo de Santa María

VALETTA, MALTA
Colección Bonelli
Museo de la Co-Catedral de San Juan

ESTADOS UNIDOS

NEW YORK Metropolitan Museum	**PRINCETON** Bárbara P. Johnson Collection	**HARTFORD** Ateneo Wassworth
KANSAS CITY Atkins Museum	**CLEVELAND** Museum of Art	**DETROI** Detroit Institute of Art

FORT WORTH
Museum Kimbell

CRONOLOGÍA

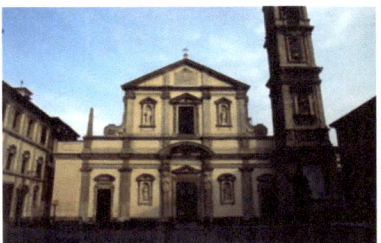
BASÍLICA DE S. ETTIENNE, MILÁN

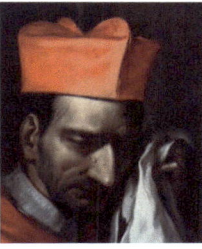
CARLO BORROMEO

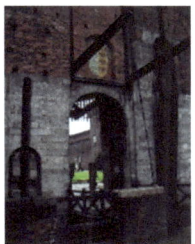
CASTILLO SFORZA, MILÁN

1571. Michelangelo Merisi da Caravaggio nace en Milán el 29 de septiembre, hijo de Fermo Merisi, arquitecto, supervisor y administrador de las propiedades de Francesco Sforza, que fuera testigo de su boda con Lucía Aratori, emparentada a su vez con la joven marquesa Constanza Colonna, hija del almirante Marcoantonio Colonna, cuya fama culminó en 1571 con la victoria de Lepanto, recién casada con Francesco. Caravaggio fue bautizado ese mismo año en la Basílica de San Ettienne en Milán.

1576. Milán se ve asolada por la plaga y los Merisi se trasladan para Caravaggio, donde alrededor de ese año, víctimas de la misma, mueren su padre, su abuelo y su tío. Carlo Borromeo (1538-1584), Arzobispo de Milán, con sus rígidas medidas eclesiásticas, instrucciones específicas sobre la ornamentación de las iglesias, la austeridad y la misericordia permea el discurso oficial de la Contrarreforma durante los años de formación de Caravaggio.

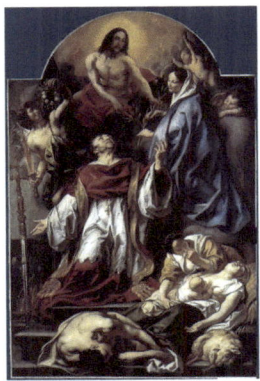
JACOB JORDAENS: LA PLAGA, INTERCESIÓN DE BORROMEO

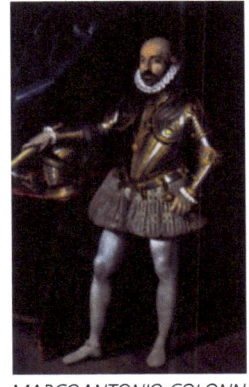
MARCOANTONIO COLONNA HÉROE DE LEPANTO

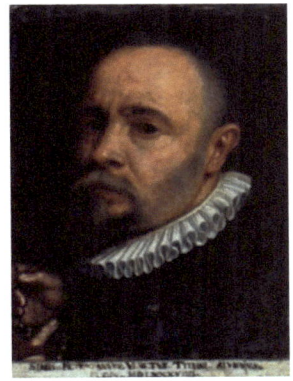
SIMONE PETEREZANO AUTORRETRATO

1584-1588. Por gestiones de su madre, se firma un contrato con Simone Peterzano para que Caravaggio lleve a efecto su aprendizaje como pintor, que terminará en 1588. Se ignoran los detalles específicos de su vida en Milán, donde, por un lado, imperaba el fanatismo religioso y por el otro era una ciudad turbulenta donde predominaban la violencia, los robos y los homicidios, la prostitución, la promiscuidad, las bandas callejeras y toda clase de vicios. Es posibles que el propio Caravaggio estuviera envuelto en actos delictivos, aunque los hechos no están documentados.

1590. Muere Lucía Aratori. Se reparten los bienes familiares.

ROMA

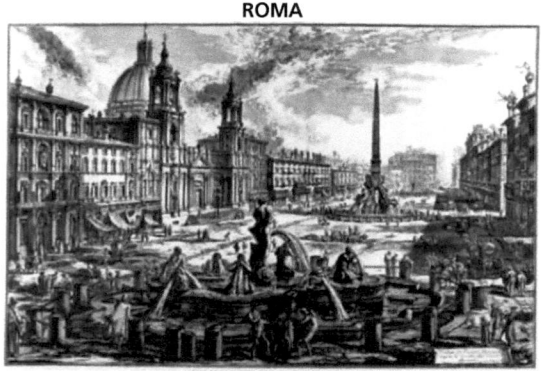

GIOVANNI BATISTA PIRANESI, PLAZA NAVONA

1592-1593. Caravaggio llega a Roma. Clemente VIII, el nuevo Papa, asciende al poder. Seguramente Caravaggio queda impresionado por la grandiosidad de Roma, bajo el auspicio del Papa, y se integra a la vida metropolitana. Predominan la pobreza, el bandidaje y la delincuencia, en un ambiente de total desmoralización, pero dentro de un contexto arquitectónico monumental y de grandes palacios. Durante esos años la pasa muy mal, y en un principio se tiene que poner al servicio de monseñor Pandolfo Pucci copiando cuadros devocionales y pasando hambre.

La incesante comidilla diaria entre los romanos, escándalos, insultos, difamaciones, se daban a conocer en la plaza pública a través de noticias anónimas que se publicaban debajo de la estatua del "Pasquino", que representaban la voz pública como si fuera un "twiter" electrónico contemporáneo, cuyas consecuencias específicas llevarán al episodio legal entre Baglione y Caravaggio.

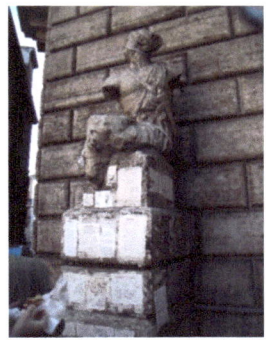 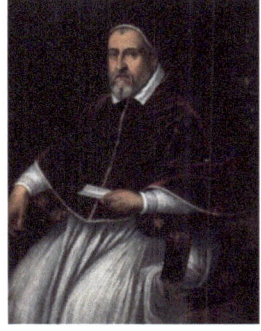 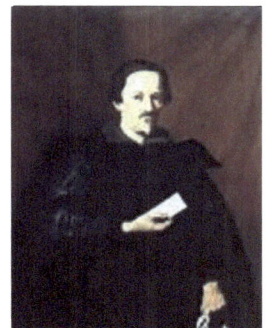

EL PASQUINO   *CLEMENTE VIII*   *VINCENZO GUISTINIANI*

1593-1594. Sin dirección fija, hambriento y necesitado, vive en pésimas condiciones y se ve precisado a trabajar en el taller de Guiseppe Cesari, Cavaliere D'Arpino, donde sólo podía pintar flores y frutas, en una posición humillante. Entre otros percances, Merisi recibe la pateadura de un caballo y pasa un tiempo en el Hospital de la Consolación. Se enferma. Conoce a Mario Minniti (1577-1640) que se convertirá en su mejor amigo. Cuando sale del hospital no regresa a trabajar con los hermanos Cesari. Al iniciarse la amistad con Minniti, que le va servir de modelo, viven juntos y pinta de forma independiente por varios años.

1594-1595. A través de Constantino Spata, conocido como Maestro Valentino, que compraba y revendía cuadros junto a la iglesia de San Luigui, entra en contacto con el que será su protector, el cardenal del Monte, que compra *La buenaventura* y *Partida de cartas*. Bajo su protección su suerte cambia y pasa a vivir hasta 1601 en el Palacio Madama, donde recibe mesa y mesada. Al mismo tiempo, se acrecienta su vida callejera con sus correspondientes trifulcas y encuentros con la policía que llevan a que lo encarcelen en la Tor di Nona.

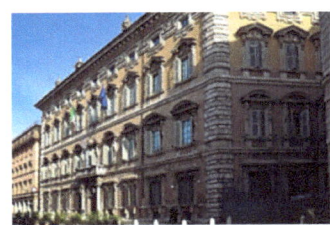 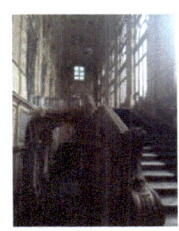 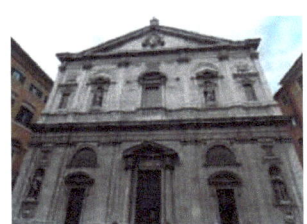

PALACIO MADAMA   *P. MADAMA*   *SAN LUIS DE LOS FRANCESES*

1597. Misterioso episodio con Pietropaolo, mozo de un barbero, que nunca quedó debidamente aclarado, cerca de San Agustín. Se incrementan las relaciones con sus compinches de juergas, y con las prostitutas y cortesanas del Ortazio. Ana Bianchini y Fillis Melandroni, entre doce y catorce años, posan para Caravaggio.

1599. Ejecución de Beatriz Cenci y su familia.

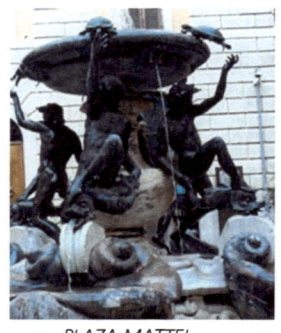
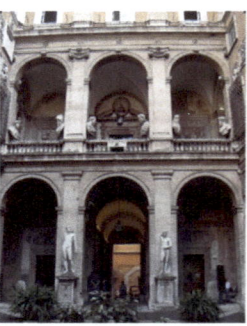

GIORDANO BRUNO   *PLAZA MATTEI*   *PALACIO MATTEI*

1600. Año de éxitos y de violencia. Un millón de peregrinos llega a Roma. Giordano Bruno es condenado por Clemente VIII a morir en la hoguera en el Campo de Fiori. Caravaggio termina su trabajo en la Capilla Contarelli en San Luigi. Lo comisionan para pintar dos cuadros en la capilla Cerasi en Santa María del Popolo. Se incrementan su irritabilidad y sus trifulcas. Los archivos policíacos dejan constancia de adicionales peleas de Onorio Longhi con Tomassoni en la cancha de tenis, con supuesta participación de Caravaggio, y se indica que Merisi estaba convaleciente de una enfermedad. Intervención de la policía. Episodio cerca de la calle Scrofa, donde Longi, inseparable compañero de juergas, provoca a las fuerzas policíacas con toda clase de palabrotas. Ataque nocturno de Merisi a Girolamo Spampa que conduce a un proceso legal. Correlación contradictoria entre la violencia y los éxitos de Caravaggio como pintor.

1601. Caravaggio termina de pintar *La conversión de San Pablo* I y II. Cecco Boneri modela para Caravaggio por primera vez. Annibale Carraci, que termina de decorar el Palacio Farnesio y muestras graves signos de inestabilidad mental, se expresa despectivamente de la obra de Merisi.

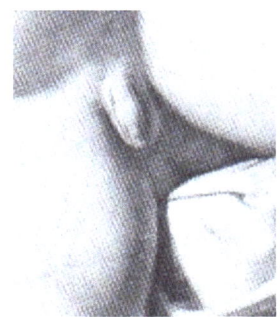 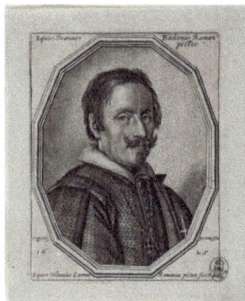 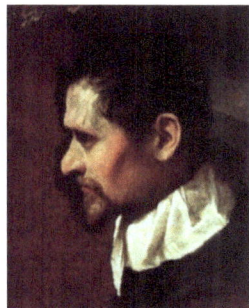

CECCO BONERI *GIOVANNI BAGLIONE* *ANNIBALE CARRACCI*

1602. Caravaggio pinta los genitales de Cecco Boneri en *Amor Victorioso*, que Vincenzo Giustiniani exhibe en su colección privada. Ese mismo año los vuelve a pintar haciendo de San Juan Bautista, como regalo que le hace Ciriaco Mattei a su hijo con motivo de su cumpleaños en el cual Caravaggio es igualmente explícito, variantes ambos de un mismo discurso transgresor. Por otro lado, le rechazan San Mateo I y le aceptan una segunda versión con un ángel a lo Cecco Bonneri. Apogeo de su relación con Cecco.

1603. Auge de la violencia. Con motivo del juicio entablado por Guiovanni Baglione, su enemigo más pertinaz, Caravaggio tiene que interrumpir *El sacrificio de Isaac*. Arrestado en la Plaza Navona lo encarcelan por un par de semanas entre agosto y septiembre. Al ser condenado por difamación, sufre prisión domiciliaria y le alquila una casa de dos pisos, patio, buhardilla y sótano a Prudencia Bruni en la calle San Biagio en el Campo Marzio. Violento episodio de las alcachofas que le tira al camarero en la Hostería del Moro.

1604. Relación con Lena Antognetti, que le servirá de modelo para *La Virgen de los peregrinos* y *La Virgen de los palafreneros*. A los efectos de lograr una luz cenital abre un boquete en el techo del estudio en el cual trabajaba. Como apunta Robb: "La oscuridad era el medio onírico en el que nadaban las imágenes y encubría la falta de lógica que vinculaba esas cosas en la mente… Hacía su arte cada vez más difícil, exigiendo una mayor participación del observador, obligándolo a esforzarse por ver en la creciente oscuridad…". Dos nuevos encarcelamientos durante los últimos meses del año, con el agravante de llamar "chupa vergas" al oficial que lo arrestó, lo cual da la medida del estado en que se encontraba.

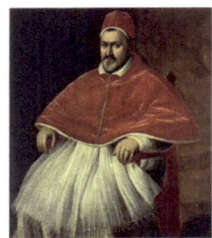 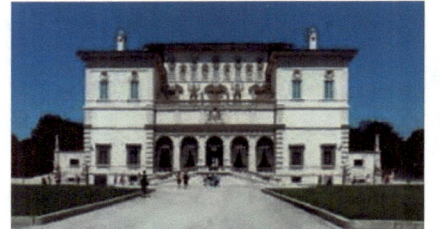 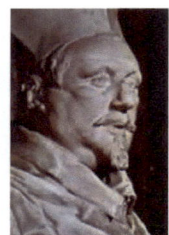

PABLO V BORGHESE   *PALACIO BORGHESE*   *SCIPIANO BORGEHESE*

1605. El notario Pancracio Pasqualone denuncia a Caravaggio por haberlo atacado violentamente en la Plaza Navona por supuestos atrevimientos con Lena. En el Palacio del Quirinal firma un acuerdo de paz con Pasqualone. La relación sexual con Lena parece dejar sentada la orientación sexual de Caravaggio con el sexo opuesto, aunque no excluye a Cecco. Caravaggio tiene nuevos enfrentamientos con la policía. Se acrecienta el sadomasoquismo en su vida y obra. Viaje a Génova bajo la protección de Constanza Colonna, que va a jugar un papel cada vez más importante en su vida. Regreso a Roma. Acuerdo judicial que lo obliga a hacer las paces con Pasqualone. Se hace un inventario de sus propiedades y se le confiscan las mismas. Por falta de pago, se le prohíbe que siga viviendo en la casa del callejón de San Biagio. Se inicia su relación profesional con Scipione Borghese y con su tío, Pablo V Borghese que residen en el Palacio del Quirinal, sede del poder. Scipione le extorsiona *San Jerónimo escribiendo*. Retrata a Pablo V. Es herido en la garganta y en una oreja en una pelea callejera.

1606. Retiran *La Virgen de los palafreneros* de San Pedro. Le rechazan *La muerte de la Virgen*. Grandes festividades por celebrarse el primer año del papado de Pablo V. 28 de mayo: duelo a muerte con Ranuccio Tomassoni en el Campo Marcio. Caravaggio recibe heridas serias y huye a Paliano. Condenado a la pena capital por la muerte de Tomassoni, escapa a Nápoles bajo la protección de los Colonna.

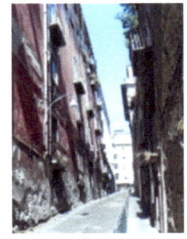 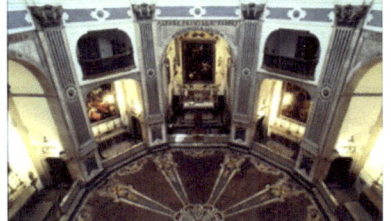 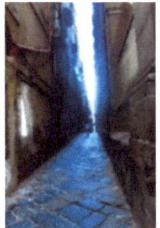

NÁPOLES.   PÍO MONTE DE LA MISERICORDIA   NÁPOLES

1607. Estancia en Nápoles. Bien acogido por los napolitanos reciben varias comisiones importantes, como le pasará después en Malta y Sicilia. Termina de pintar para el Pío Monte de la Misericordia las *Siete obras de la Misericordia* en la Vía del Tribunal. Pinta *David con la cabeza de Goliat*, que será el último cuadro en que aparece Cecco, más radiante que nunca, con la cabeza de Goliat en la mano que es un autorretrato de Caravaggio. Se incrementa el tema del martirologio cristiano y pinta en abundancia. Reanuda sus contactos con Fabrizio Sforza Colonna, el segundo hijo de Constanza Colonna, que lo aloja en su palacio, y lo ayuda para que se vaya a Malta.

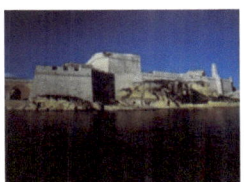 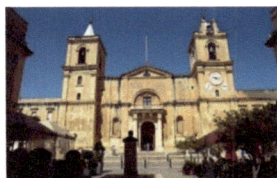 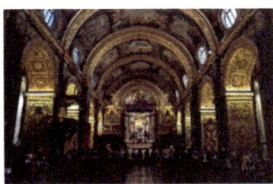

VALETA, MALTA   CASTILLO DE SAN ÁNGELO   CO-CATEDRAL

1608. Malta. Cae bajo la protección del Gran Maestre Alof de Wignacourt. Pinta *La decapitación de San Bautista*. Es nombrado Caballero de la Orden de Malta. Logra su objetivo de salir de los límites de su marginación social, pero de inmediato cae en desgracia por haber infringido uno de sus estatutos, aunque las verdaderas razones se desconocen. Lo encierran en la *guva*, de la que se ignora como pudo escapar. Es expulsado de la Orden por ser un "miembro" pútrido y pestilente. Huye a Siracusa. Rencuentro con Mario Minnitti. Visita unas cuevas monumentales y las bautiza como la Oreja del Sordo.

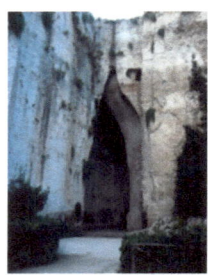 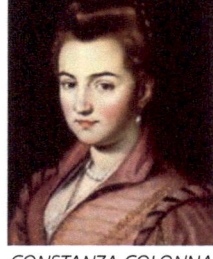 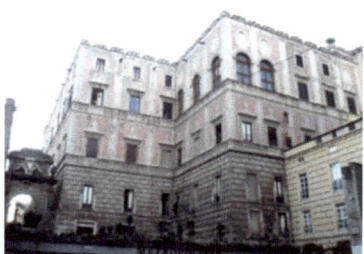

LA OREJA DEL SORDO   *CONSTANZA COLONNA*   *PALACIO COLONNA EN CELLAMARE.*

1609. Breves estancias en Mesina y Palermo. Regreso a Nápoles. Recibe la protección de Constanza Colonna y se aloja en el Palazo de Cellamare en la Vía Chiaia junto a la bahía. Atacado, herido y desfigurado en una emboscada que sufre en la Locanda del Cerriglio, de fama dudosa, donde por poco lo matan.

1610. Es perdonado por el Papa. Sale de Nápoles en una falúa, con cuatro de sus cuadros, con destino a Roma. Viaja con un salvoconducto. En Palo, un pequeño pueblo cerca de Civitavecchia, lo encarcelan por un breve período de tiempo, pero el suficiente para que la falúa zarpara nuevamente, llevándose sus cuadros. Abandonado, sólo y desesperado, corre por terrenos insalubres y peligrosos siguiendo a la embarcación a Puerto Ercole. Enferma, es hospitalizado y muere, posiblemente el 18 de julio. Se crea una teoría conspirativa, donde se establece la posibilidad, que no ha sido documentada, entra realidad y ficción, de que fuera asesinado.

PUERTO ERCOLE

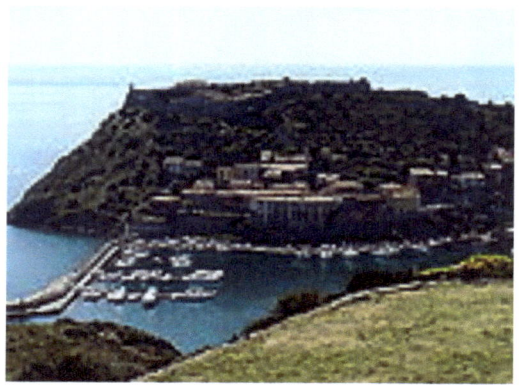

ÍNDICE

5	Palabras preliminares
9	Libro Primero
23	Libro Segundo
44	Itinerario pictórico
47	Museos, altares y galerías
49	Cronología

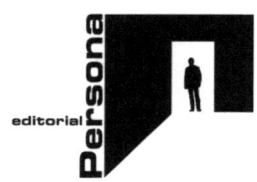

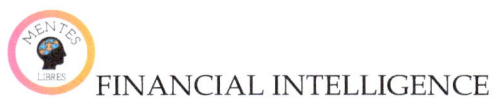

FINANCIAL INTELLIGENCE

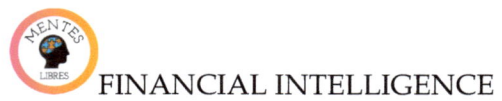
FINANCIAL INTELLIGENCE

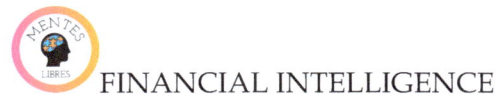 FINANCIAL INTELLIGENCE

INDEX

You'll get the same

What is money?

Before the change…

Time and money

Ways to Reach Wealth

Main rule for investing

How to get out of a financial mess

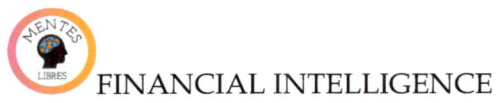FINANCIAL INTELLIGENCE

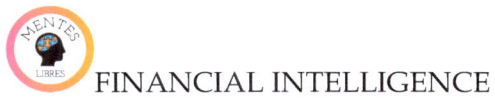
FINANCIAL INTELLIGENCE

You'll get the same

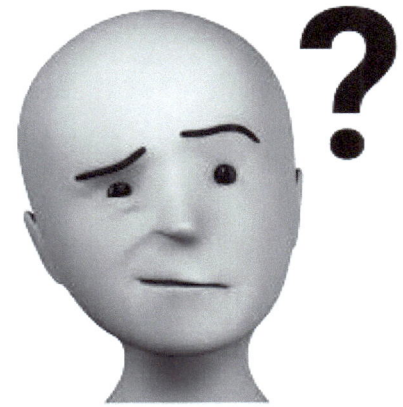

Naturally, most of us, if not all of us, want and long for something better. It is part of us if we want a bigger car, a better house; buy good things for the family. We're still waiting for more, but to get what you don't have, you have to do something you've never done

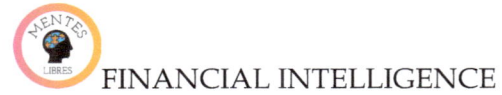
FINANCIAL INTELLIGENCE

before.

That simply means:

Doing the same thing over and over again expecting different results! **CRAZY!!!!!!!**

As an employee, you can't stay in the same job forever and expect a miracle to happen and your boss to suddenly give you a raise. You will be lucky that there is no downsizing in your company. Switching to another company will only provide a short-term solution to a long-term problem.

Sure, you can take a second or even third job, but do you have enough hours and stamina in a day to keep it up?

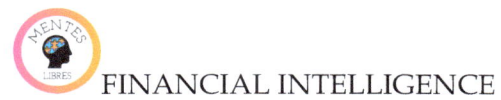 FINANCIAL INTELLIGENCE

The bottom line: Exchanging time for money is not a good long-term financial sense. You keep increasing the hours just to win the rat race. That never leads to extraordinary results.

Raising their wages only puts them at a higher tax level. Their wages increase, but so do their household and auto expenses. How are you going to invest in yourself when all the time you spend working for a company, working for the government paying taxes and working for the bank paying for your house and car?

What if you get sick and can't work tomorrow? Will the government take care of your family?

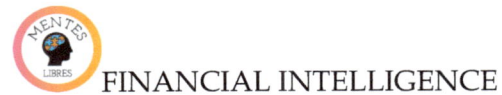FINANCIAL INTELLIGENCE

I very much doubt it.

Isn't it time you took finances a little more seriously?

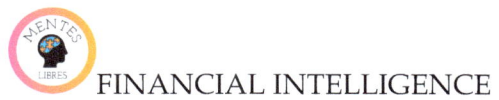

What is money?

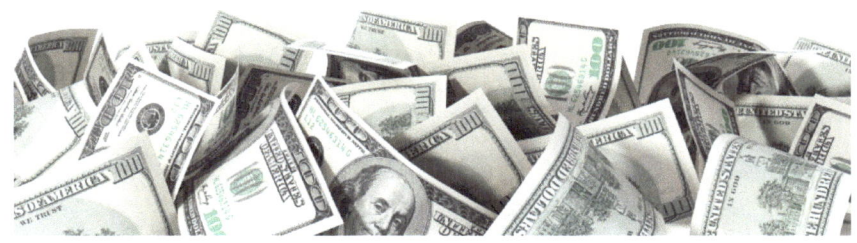

You see, there are a lot of ideas of what people think money is.

Some say it's a form of measurement.

Yes, but a measure of what? Wealth? In the old days, people measured wealth by the

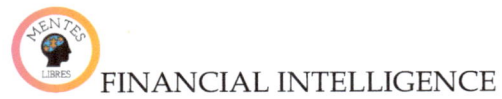

number of cows, sheep, and horses they had. But do people today measure wealth by their cows and horses? What about slaves? Was there a time when labor was considered a hot commodity? Are slaves worth anything today? Is your money sitting in the bank to protect it if a recession hits the country? No, wealth cannot be measured by the base dollar.

Some say it is a form of power.

Yes, money can give you power, but if you are trapped on a deserted island forever with a great treasure, will that money mean anything to you? If someone offered you water and a helicopter to fly out of there, you would exchange all your money in a fraction of a second, so money is not a precise measure of power - it depends to a great

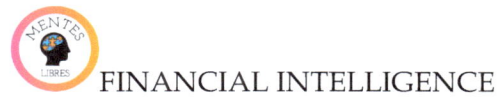

extent on how and wisely you use it!

Many believe that it is the root of all evil... and many others assume this belief without much questioning.

Now, now, now, now... money is NOT the root of all evil (otherwise, why do you think churches still accept monetary donations and charity?). The love of money is the root of evil. Remember, money is an excellent servant, but a terrible master. If you are trading your life for money, money has power over your time and your life.

And unless you have the right financial information, lack of money can engender a lot of evil thoughts and a negative mentality, as seen mainly in cheats, thieves, criminals,

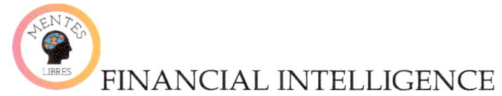 FINANCIAL INTELLIGENCE

breakups, scroungers, stingy, and more, to name a few.

But what is money really?

Money is an idea, backed by trust.

While money has been developed naturally by merchants in the old days to replace the questionable barter system, money today is literally invented by the rich and rich.

Entrepreneurs are willing to get rid of their money to buy other people's time. The time of other people, i.e. employees and the self-employed, becomes the asset of their employer and employers this invaluable resource to continue creating more wealth for

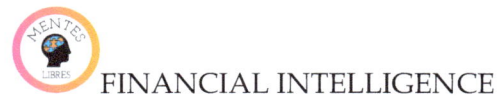 FINANCIAL INTELLIGENCE

themselves.

And here's the thing: while you work for money, you're enslaved by it!

90% of today's population is being involuntarily enslaved.

What we don't realize is that there is a part of our soul that cannot be bought at any price. Would you cut off your little finger if your boss offered you 24 months of your salary immediately? You and I know we're worth more than that. But when you hear of people selling their body parts for cash in some countries, we can make our eyes pop out of orbits.

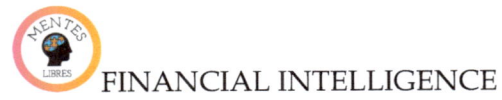FINANCIAL INTELLIGENCE

On the other hand, we occasionally sell a part of ourselves for money like a donkey and a carrot.

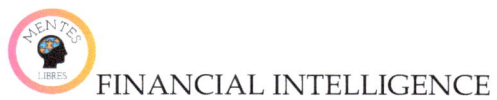 FINANCIAL INTELLIGENCE

Before the change...

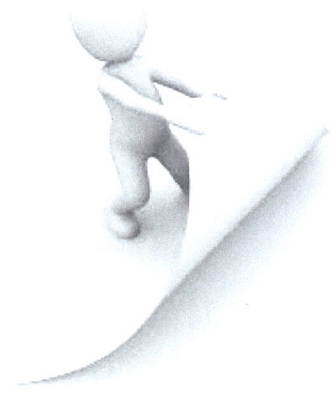

Now don't get me wrong: I'm not working on a job (I worked on one before I became an **ENTREPRENEUR**).

But let's face it: our current needs grow more

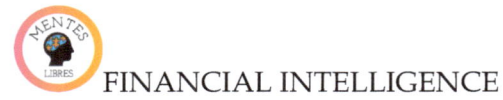 FINANCIAL INTELLIGENCE

than ever in any period of history. Prices go up, wages don't. There are more **baby boomers** than ever and they have very little pension to show for their decades of hard work.

And you can't guess how many people hate the unhealthy, hectic lifestyle of getting up early, dealing with stress for most of the day, joining traffic jams, spending more money and time traveling, enjoying very little rest, and repeating the viscosity cycle.

You definitely don't paint a good financial and lifestyle picture, do you?

The first step to change is to be aware of the problem. Awareness before change (or ABC for short) is necessary if you are going to

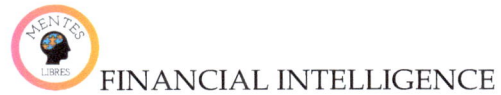

make some change in life to start taking control of your financial life and then get out of the rat race.

We need consciousness to know what state we're in so we know where we're going.

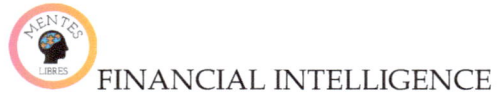 FINANCIAL INTELLIGENCE

Time and money

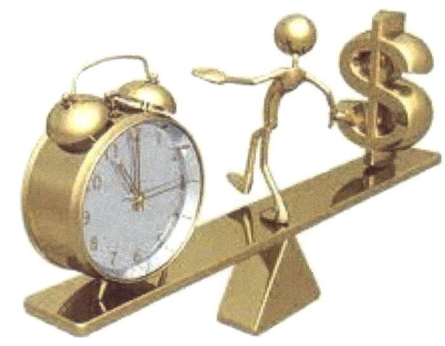

There are 4 types of people in the world:

1. **No time, no money.**

Most employees fall into this category. You

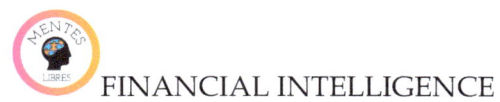
FINANCIAL INTELLIGENCE

can't go shopping on a Tuesday afternoon or fire your boss whenever you want. Most employees can't even save money on their pension for 3 years!

2. No time, lots of money.

Self-employed, professional and small business owners are in this category.

They are a little better off than the employee because they earn more, but they have to work even harder than the employees to keep up with declining profit margins, competition and service to their customers.

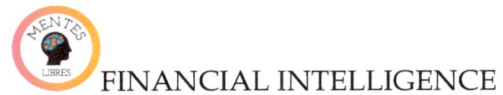 FINANCIAL INTELLIGENCE

3. I have time, I don't have money.

Many farmers, school dropouts or vagrants have a lot of time but no money. Perhaps ignorance is a blessing, but without a stable source of income, how long can you last in the future?

4. I have time and a lot of money.

It is the category in which large entrepreneurs, owners and investors find themselves. Imagine, not having to work for money, but having money to work for you by investing it and making a profit by using your money to make money. **GLOORIOUS**!!!!!!!!!

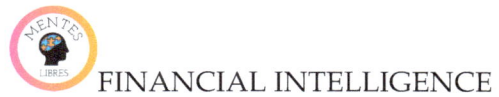 FINANCIAL INTELLIGENCE

Now ask yourself?

1. Which of the four categories do you currently fall into?

2. What category do you want to be in tomorrow?

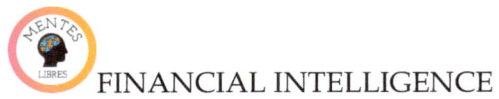
FINANCIAL INTELLIGENCE

Ways to Reach Wealth

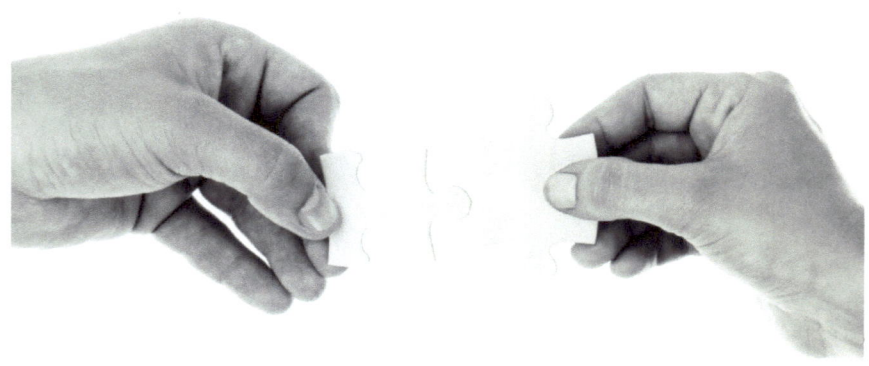

2 Models of wealth creation

Everyone wants to earn more money, but people in general and is divided into two categories:

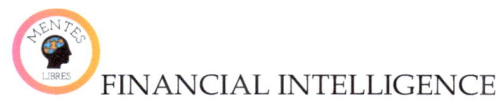
FINANCIAL INTELLIGENCE

- Those who bring results after they are promised wealth first or those who bring results first, are then rewarded by others later. (EMPLOYED AND SELF-EMPLOYED).

- Those, entrepreneurs, business owners and investors.

There is no good or bad in this kind of thinking, but keep in mind: once again, you are trading your precious time for money. Instead of investing your time in an ASSET that generates money, you spend your time working on something that is short-term, of limited wealth, and does not give you much income after you stop working.

Also consider that this type of short-term

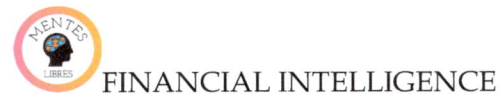 FINANCIAL INTELLIGENCE

vision will only produce limited or temporary results at best. Have you ever seen a security guard asleep at work when the boss is away?

In addition, the part where our emotions get the better of us is when at least our lives must be governed by the pursuit of the dollar. It is clear that when an employee is offered a higher salary, more medical benefits and longer vacations, his heart starts pumping faster.

A higher salary does not mean fewer financial problems. On the contrary, when your income increases, your commitments, your tax level, and the time you spend in your business increase. The higher your salary, the weaker your position will be because if your boss is paying you 5-digit

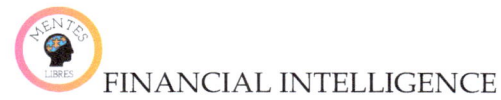

income and calls for an emergency meeting, you'd better hurry to the office even if you're halfway through making love to your wife!

I think the best definition of an employee/boss relationship can be summed up like this.

An employee will only do the minimum to prevent the boss from firing them and a boss will only pay the minimum to prevent the employee from leaving.

Now let's explore the other group…

There are many creative people, inventors, entrepreneurs and business leaders who fall into this category.

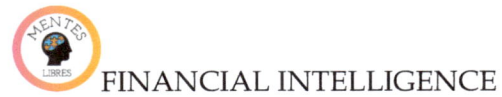
FINANCIAL INTELLIGENCE

An entrepreneur is someone who always has good ideas.

The first obstacle we have to overcome if we want to succeed in the second group is to stop working for money. What does this mean? Isn't making money part of having a good financial IQ?

What I mean by 'stop working for money' is that it's not working for free. Rather, it means working to gain the skills necessary to be a successful entreprener (or inventor, investor).

If you don't have contacts to run a business, where would be the best place to look for contacts? Of course, the customers of your

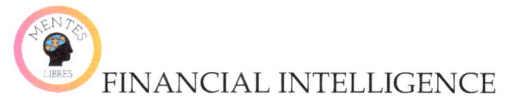
FINANCIAL INTELLIGENCE

competition.

What about product knowledge? Then work with a company that will teach you all the ins and outs of the tricks of the trade.

Not familiar with a factory production line? Work on one! Learn how to handle ropes or how to handle factory workers.

Afraid to talk to people? Get a sales job where you'll be forced to talk to a lot of people. It's also a great way to develop perseverance!

Don't you know that the best education you can get is in real life? Not in the conference room.

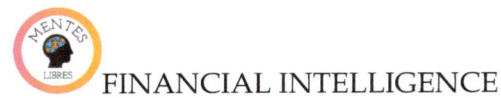

The bottom line is that not everyone has what it takes to succeed as an entrepreneur.

It's not that easy. Many lack the perseverance, creative mentality, financial capabilities or people needed to do the job and usually give up too soon before the results can be seen. The quickest way to make those skills successful is to learn them hands-on and even get paid in the process! Don't be absorbed by what they pay you.

Again, let me emphasize:

Would you trade time for money in the short term? (Money stops coming when you stop) or Trade time and money for a long-term

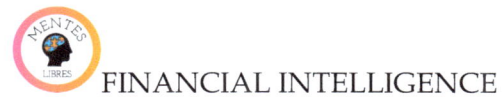 FINANCIAL INTELLIGENCE

asset that generates income? (Even long after you stopped)

God created us with a brain. All we have to do is look around us and observe the problems that need to be overcome because every problem is an opportunity in disguise.

Everything depends on you. You may or may not see results in the short term, but by using our brains and the resources that surround us, we can create real value that others are willing to pay for what we have to offer.

3 Ways to Make Money

Let me summarize the 3 ways to make money

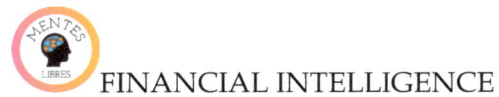
FINANCIAL INTELLIGENCE

1. Trading time for money - employee, self-employed worker

2. Manifestation and use of creative ideas - inventors, artists, programmers

3. If you are a professional, have you ever explored the possibility of writing an e-book about your field of expertise? If well written, it could provide a new source of income, rather than having you spends your time serving your clients.

What about a computer programmer? You can come up with your own revolutionary product instead of selling your ideas to the company you work for.

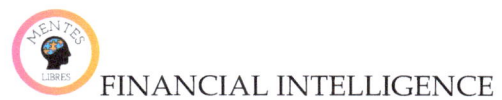 FINANCIAL INTELLIGENCE

What about real estate, rather than selling homes, you can pool sources of financing to buy cheap homes, increase their value, and sell them at a higher price. It only takes a little time and research to find good ideas.

Is money a problem? Look for loans if you can take the risk. Gather money from many investors or look for a subsidy. The sky is the limit when it comes to making money.

Again, how do you want to get wealth? Answer: It's up to you.

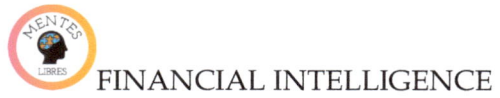 FINANCIAL INTELLIGENCE

Main rule for investing

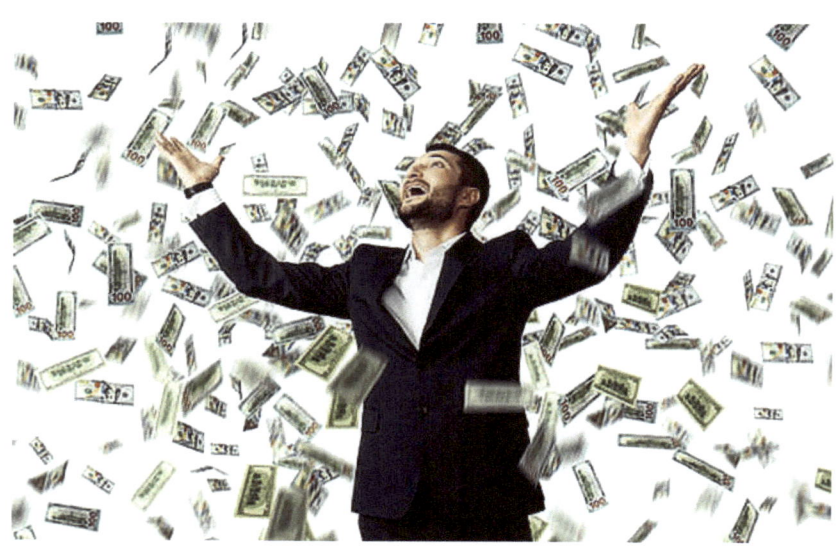

What does investing mean for people?

What comes to mind when you mention the word investment?

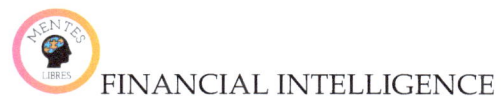
FINANCIAL INTELLIGENCE

Does it mean putting your money into insurance, mutual funds, the stock market, or even high-yield investments?

Other people only think about investing when they are about to die and have left nothing for their offspring.

Some even tremble when they hear the word, often stating that they have no money to invest or that they feel it is too complicated an issue to discuss.

Many people even invest a lot in health supplements, personal trainers and beauticians to live longer, be healthier or even look younger. Imagine the advertising

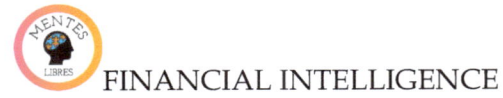 FINANCIAL INTELLIGENCE

budget of today's beauty companies.

These are all legitimate concerns when it comes to investing, but I'm talking about the most important investment a person can make in their life.

Invest in Yourself

The most important and primordial rule is "Invest in yourself" - if you don't, who else will?

Your parents will only invest in your education until you leave college. But that's just the basic needs provided and it doesn't teach you important lessons about financial education.

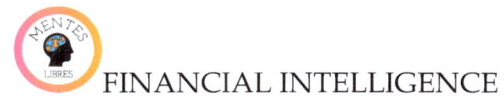FINANCIAL INTELLIGENCE

Would you depend on colleges to teach you how to make money? Most colleges only teach you skills so you can earn money by working for other people. What about business school? Honestly, if business professors are such business experts, why do they still teach there instead of making a fortune in business?

Would your boss teach you to succeed in business so that one day you'll be in their position?

You and only you have to be proactive enough to take that responsibility. You see, when you invest in yourself, it means assuming the importance of educating yourself. Education is not in the academic or

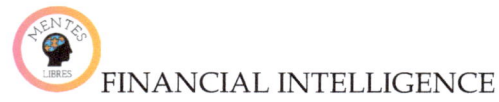 FINANCIAL INTELLIGENCE

technical sense, although they are necessary skills to be developed in life. Our education does not stop at the university.

For most working adults, their education enters a delay stage after leaving school. They stop learning and therefore stop growing. They only grow sideways by eating too many pizzas or take-away food during their busy lunch breaks.

We know IQ is important, don't we? But why aren't the world's smartest people the richest in the world? There are many accountants and financial planners running to their cars every night trying to overcome traffic jams after work! **They are not rich!**

What about Emotional Intelligence or

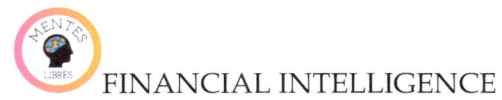

Emotional Coefficient? Do working hard, having a great attitude and a positive mentality solve our financial situation? These are important when running a business, but let me use them:

If you're driving from Boston to New York using the wrong road map, you won't get to our destination no matter how fast you drive your car (working hard!). You can work harder, but you'll only get to the wrong destination faster. You may have the best attitude in the world or the most positive mentality, but you still won't make it to New York (although the trip wouldn't bother you since you feel positive about it).

The importance of financial education You should invest FIRST in your financial IQ.

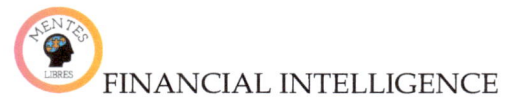 FINANCIAL INTELLIGENCE

Having a good financial IQ is not about saving tons of money or depositing it in mutual funds. It's developing a healthy money relationship and building a wealth of assets that will generate money for you.

What is needed to develop your financial IQ?

Delayed gratification is one of the most important aspects for the development of your financial IQ. Let's take this as a hypothetical example.

Would you pay for a pint of milk or a cow?

If you buy milk, it is consumed and it is over. You will have to buy the milk over and over

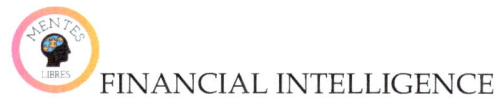

again when it is finished. Even if milk costs less than a cow, in the long run you will continue to buy milk over and over again.

Now, if a cow cost 50 times more than milk, you could pay for the nose when you buy the cow, but after consuming 50 pints of milk from the cow, you would reach the break-even point in your investment and save more money in the future. In fact, the cow could give birth to 2 or more calves and you could select one of them for profit!

Got the idea?

EVERYONE is capable of creating wealth. When you take an old car and give it a general overhaul, paint it with a new coat of paint, and change a few more parts to get it working again, you could select that car for more money than if it were just an old, ramshackle car. You would have created wealth in the process!

How about a farm? If you turned a farm into a holiday resort in the countryside, wouldn't it increase the value of farmland?

It's the same principle for cooks, computer programmers and craftsmen. The sum of the whole is greater than the parts. We are all capable of creating wealth even out of nothing and that is the first step to making our creative juices flow.

The value of anything is defined by supply and demand.

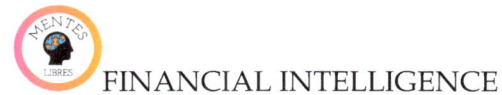
FINANCIAL INTELLIGENCE

You don't need a bachelor's degree in economics to understand this. Money is just an idea.

Remember the example of the desert island? The real measure of money is not the cents or dollars it represents.

If you have developed a product that people want, would you pay them more than usual? Would you apply your skills to create good assets?

The bottom line is this:

Invest in assets that add long-term value. Anything that brings you more income is an advantage. Don't invest too much in liabilities like cars or boats.

(If you lost your job tomorrow and can't pay for your house, is your house an asset or a liability?) Are you willing to leave your comfort zone and pay the price of the financial IQ? Or ignore the signs of the times and expect your boss, government and bank to take financial care of you for the rest of your life, living below your means and never taking risks to improve your family's future?.

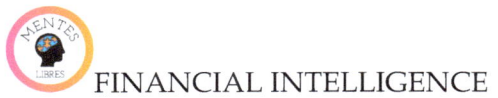
FINANCIAL INTELLIGENCE

How to get out of a financial mess

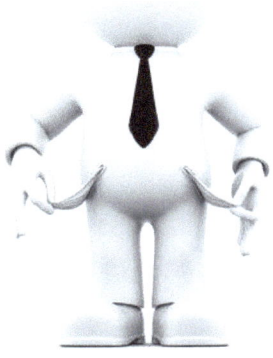

There are two methods I can recommend to get out of a financial mess.

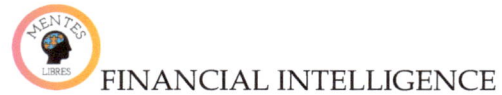
FINANCIAL INTELLIGENCE

Defensive Strategies

The first is defensive:

Reduce what you are already spending. You can't start a business in a financial mess. Cash flow is more important than income. And you need to have a lot of cash flow out of your pockets if you want to succeed.

Here are some of the things you can reduce

- Smoking - if you can't quit, simply reduce your consumption of a few cigarettes.

- Alcohol - alcohol can drain your finances faster than a running faucet.

- Night out - spending a few nights at home thinking about making more money.

- Betting - if you plan to bet, it's better to bet on a business.

- Vacation and country clubs - you won't die without a few memberships.

- Food - eat healthy and you can think more clearly.

- Laziness - the biggest thing that will stop you!

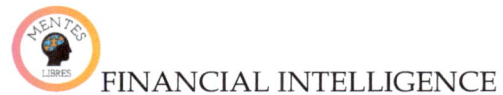 FINANCIAL INTELLIGENCE

The most important thing of all is that you don't buy anything that constitutes a risk. A liability is anything that takes money out of your pocket no matter what it's worth in the future. Think in terms of cash flow. What can I invest in today to raise funds tomorrow?

Now let's move on to offensive strategies:

Offensive Strategies

One of the best, low-cost ways to invest in your business skills is to join a network marketing company. There are many other options, such as starting a traditional business or even an online business.

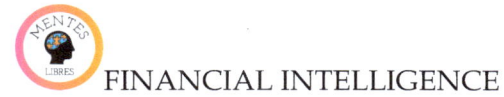
FINANCIAL INTELLIGENCE

But if you want to guarantee something concrete where business skills are a concern, my opinion is about Network Marketing.

Regardless of what you've heard about this industry or how much money people have lost there, the main reason I would recommend everyone to invest in a network marketing company is because of what you can learn there, and not because of the amount of money you can make (although it would be fantastic if you can make a living from it).

You see, network marketing companies are the only place where people share their trade secrets for **FREE**. It's logical because for your bottom line to succeed, they'll also want you to succeed! Therefore, they will not refrain from teaching you the skills of a

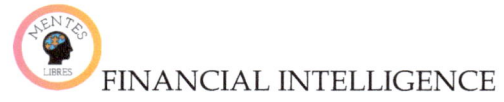

businessman.

In addition, the relatively low cost of investing in a network marketing company will surprise you by what you can learn from the price you are paying (a few bottles of vitamins and a business kit for the experience of a lifetime!). They patiently train you in the business attitudes and skills you need to succeed in this industry.

Basically, you can't succeed in network marketing with an employee's mentality. A network marketing company will train you in sales, communication, teamwork, leadership, positive thinking, self-improvement, investment of time and money, as well as the support of your up line as a personal trainer and mentor. I dare say that even if you don't earn a penny, but have diligently participated in their program, the skills you develop will last a lifetime.

You can also develop skills by linking up with an insurance agency. The work can be very hard, but those companies will also teach you the same skills as the previous ones and may also give you some advice on financial planning.

How about an Internet business? If you are computer literate, Internet businesses offer a low-cost, high-margin business that can earn a lot of money and access a global market.

Other places where you can learn about business skills can be found in financial planning courses, real estate investment courses, time management courses and much

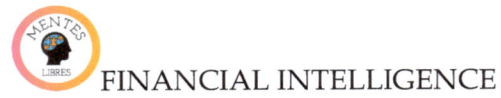 FINANCIAL INTELLIGENCE

more.

All this I have suggested will be the safest way to start a new business. You are only spending a few hundred to thousands of dollars on start-up and education.

A traditional business can be too risky for someone without commercial experience.

You invest tens of thousands of dollars and may have difficulty getting to the break-even point. But once you've developed the skills above, you'll have a greater chance of success.

Most important of all, in addition to a good learning attitude, are the people you relate to.

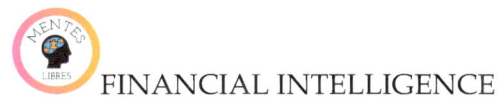 FINANCIAL INTELLIGENCE

It's been said before; you're the sum of the five people you spend the most time with!

This is very hard to swallow, but imagine if you start talking to your five beer-drinking and poker friends that you want to go out on your own and make a fortune, what would they say? They'd laugh at their socks before shattering your ego into a thousand pieces!

In the heart of man lies jealousy. They don't want to see the people around them succeed. If you succeed, it makes them look bad. They know in their hearts that they're not going anywhere, but they embrace that lifestyle and drag you along with them. They will steal your dream, and they will steal your financial freedom if you are not careful!

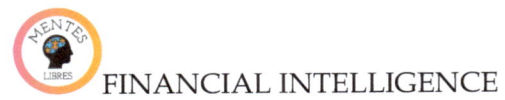 FINANCIAL INTELLIGENCE

The key point to remember is: They only mingle with positive-thinking people!

Positive thinking is not a desire. A desirous thinker is a dreamer who does not act. Positive thinking is backed by action and you will feel the energy of the people who believe in you and support your dreams.

If you walk with ducks, you will croak... but if you walk with eagles, you will rise!

So start looking for people who follow your vision or who want to grow with you.

Finally, you must **BELIEVE IN YOURSELF**!

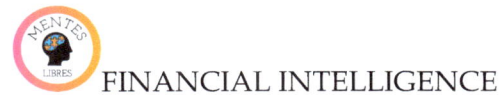 FINANCIAL INTELLIGENCE

The task of getting out of your comfort zone can seem frightening and many will not support your sleep. They may even go on the offensive even if you don't share your dream. That person may even be your parents or spouse. Then you'll face the question, is my financial freedom worth the price I'm paying now? Can I live another day with the same routine, the same job, the same pay or the same job? If the answer is no, then take action NOW. Not tomorrow, you will wake up and forget your dream.

Write your wish on a piece of paper and hold on to it firmly every day. Share it with someone positive and take the first step.

You won't regret it.

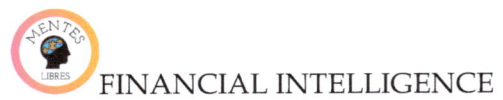 FINANCIAL INTELLIGENCE

For your financial freedom!!!

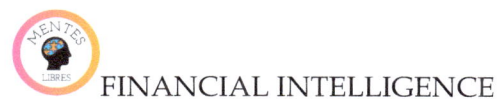 FINANCIAL INTELLIGENCE

Visit our author page on Amazon and get more MENTES LIBRES!

http://amazon.com/author/menteslibres

If you wish, you can leave a comment on this book by clicking on the following link so that we can continue to grow! Thank you very much for your purchase!

https://www.amazon.com/dp/B08265SDJ9

www.ingramcontent.com/pod-product-compliance
Lightning Source LLC
Chambersburg PA
CBHW040240220526
45473CB00001B/314